**Taxcafe Tax Guides**

# Tax-Free Cash

## By Nick Braun PhD

# Important Legal Notices:

**Published by:**
Taxcafe UK Limited
67 Milton Road
Kirkcaldy KY1 1TL
Tel: (0044) 01592 560081
Email: team@taxcafe.co.uk


1st Edition, March 2024


ISBN 978-1-911020-91-2

# Disclaimer

1.  This guide is intended as **general guidance** only and does NOT constitute accountancy, tax, financial, investment or other professional advice.

2.  The author and Taxcafe UK Limited make no representations or warranties with respect to the accuracy or completeness of this publication and cannot accept any responsibility or liability for any loss or risk, personal or otherwise, which may arise, directly or indirectly, from reliance on information contained in this publication.

3.  Please note that tax legislation, the law and practices by government and regulatory authorities (e.g. HM Revenue & Customs) are constantly changing. We recommend that for accountancy, tax, financial, investment or other professional advice, you consult a suitably qualified accountant, tax specialist, independent financial adviser, or other professional adviser.

4.  Please also note that your personal circumstances may vary from the general examples given in this guide and your professional adviser will be able to give specific advice based on your personal circumstances.

5.  This guide covers UK taxation only and any references to 'tax' or 'taxation', unless the contrary is expressly stated, refer to UK taxation only. Please note that references to the 'UK' do not include the Channel Islands or the Isle of Man. Foreign tax implications are beyond the scope of this guide.

6.  While this guide may refer to matters other than UK taxation, Taxcafe UK Limited and the author do not accept any responsibility or liability for any loss which may arise from reliance on such information contained in this guide.

7.  All persons described in the examples in this guide are entirely fictional. Any similarities to actual persons, living or dead, or to fictional characters created by any other author, are entirely coincidental.

## Dedication

To Tilly, my daughter.

## About the Author & Taxcafe

Dr Nick Braun founded Taxcafe in 1999, along with his partner Aileen Smith. As the driving force behind the company, their aim is to provide affordable plain-English tax information for private individuals, business owners and professional advisors.

Since then Taxcafe has become one of the best-known tax publishers in the UK and has won several prestigious business awards.

Nick has been a specialist tax writer since 1989, first in South Africa, where he edited the monthly *Tax Breaks* publication, and since 1999 in the UK, where he has authored several tax books including *Pension Magic*, *Small Business Tax Saving Tactics* and *Salary versus Dividends*.

Nick also has a PhD in economics from the University of Glasgow, where he was awarded the prestigious William Glen scholarship and later became a Research Fellow.

# Contents

**Introduction**     **1**

**Part 1**     **Interest Rate Basics**     **7**

**Chapter 1**  The Importance of Real Interest Rates     9

**Chapter 2**  The Financial Services Compensation Scheme     17

**Chapter 3**  The Importance of Annual Equivalent Rates     23

**Part 2**     **How Interest Income Is Taxed**     **27**

**Chapter 4**  The Personal Savings Allowance & Starting-Rate Band     29

**Chapter 5**  The Tax Rates on Interest Income     34

**Chapter 6**  When Interest Income Is Taxed     39

**Chapter 7**  Company Owners with Interest Income     44

**Part 3**     **Making the Most of Tax-Free ISAs**     **51**

**Chapter 8**  Cash ISAs     53

**Chapter 9**  Money Market Funds     60

**Chapter 10**  Cash ISA or Stocks and Shares ISA?     65

**Chapter 11**  Innovative Finance ISAs     68

**Part 4**     **More Tax Planning Ideas**     **73**

**Chapter 12**  Using Pension Contributions to Pay Less Tax     75

**Chapter 13**  Using Your Children to Save Tax     82

**Part 5**      **Savings Platforms & Premium Bonds**      **89**

**Chapter 14** Savings Platforms: Making it Easy          91
             to Enjoy the Best Interest Rates

**Chapter 15** Earn Tax-Free 'Interest' from Premium Bonds      97


**Part 6**      **Sole Traders & Company Owners**      **103**

**Chapter 16** Business Savings Accounts          105

**Chapter 17** Tax-Free Directors Loans          114


**Part 7**      **Earn Tax-Free Interest by**      **123**
             **Paying Off Your Debt**

**Chapter 18** Paying Off the Mortgage on Your Home          125

**Chapter 19** Paying Off Your Mortgage vs Tax-Free Savings          129

**Chapter 20** Paying Off Other Personal Debts          133

**Chapter 21** Paying Off Buy-to-Let Debt          135

**Chapter 22** Paying Off Business Debt          140

**Chapter 23** Company Owners with Business Premises          145

# Introduction

Between 2009 and 2022 the UK enjoyed well over a decade of rock-bottom interest rates.

Rates were first cut aggressively in the aftermath of the 2008 global financial crisis and reached their lowest level in March 2020, during the coronavirus pandemic, when the Bank of England cut its base rate to just 0.1%.

A similar picture could be seen all around the world. Some commentators pointed out that interest rates hadn't been this low in 5,000 years.

Throughout this period mortgages were dirt cheap, providing a huge boon to homeowners and landlords. At one point it was possible to fix your mortgage at less than 1% for five years.

Savers were not so lucky. Most easy-access accounts paid minuscule amounts of interest, often no more than 0.1% per year. Many people simply left all their cash in a current account earning no interest at all – there was very little incentive to do anything else.

This has all changed. The era of ultra-low interest rates is now over and savers and borrowers have to change their behaviour to make the most of the new state of affairs.

That's what this brand new guide is all about. In the pages that follow you will discover how to earn more interest on your cash and how to make sure your interest is always ***tax free***.

## Part 1 Interest Rate Basics

Chapter 1 looks at the importance of *real* (inflation-adjusted) interest rates. If you can earn a real return on your savings, your wealth will increase over time.

But to earn that precious real return you may have to shop around for the best deals AND your interest income will probably have to be tax free.

1

To enjoy the highest interest rates you may have to place your savings in some of the smaller, lesser-known banks. Fortunately the Financial Services Compensation Scheme (FSCS) shoulders all the risk – up to £85,000 per person per banking group.

Chapter 2 tells you everything you need to know about this compensation scheme: how company owners and other business owners are protected, how cash held in your SIPP or stocks and shares ISA is protected, how to avoid banks that share the same banking licence and the special protection for "temporary high balances" of up to £1 million.

Chapter 3 explains how the "annual equivalent rates" (AERs) you see advertised with various savings products are calculated and how to use them to maximise your interest income.

## Part 2 How Interest Income Is Taxed

Chapter 4 covers the personal savings allowance and starting-rate band. These allow you to earn anything from £500 to £6,000 of tax-free interest when your savings are not sheltered in an ISA.

Chapter 5 shows how much income tax is payable by those who have used up their various tax-free allowances and what can be done to reduce the amount of tax payable on interest income.

Chapter 6 explains **when** your interest income will be taxed. With some savings accounts interest is only taxable when the product matures – possibly after five years. In one example we show how, by postponing tax, the taxpayer ends up £1,469 better off; in another example the taxpayer ends up £737 worse off.

If you are a company owner you may be able to enjoy an additional £5,000 of tax-free interest. However, your interest income may also increase the tax payable on your dividend income. Chapter 7 has several examples showing how much tax different company owners pay on their interest income.

## Part 3 Making the Most of Tax-Free ISAs

We all know about ISAs but this part of the guide contains lots of unique information that will help you make the most of this wonderful tax shelter.

Chapter 8 looks at cash ISAs: how to find the highest interest rates, a recent change that has made cash ISAs much more attractive, the tremendous benefits of Flexible ISAs (not all banks offer them) and how to transfer your existing ISA savings to take advantage of the best deals.

Chapter 9 covers money market funds. These have attracted billions of pounds of investors' cash in recent times. Money market funds pay more interest than most banks (around 5.3% at present), all tax free if held in a stocks and shares ISA. However, they're also a bit more risky than conventional savings products.

In Chapter 10 we discuss whether it's better to use your £20,000 ISA allowance to earn tax-free interest in a cash ISA or tax-free capital gains and dividends in a stocks and share ISA.

Chapter 11 examines the pros and cons of Innovative Finance ISAs. These offer the opportunity to earn much more tax-free interest (maybe 10% or more) but the risks are far greater.

## Part 4 More Tax Planning Ideas

If you have to pay income tax on some of your interest income you can reduce the damage by making bigger pension contributions. Chapter 12 contains a number of examples showing how you can completely wipe out all the income tax payable on your interest income.

Chapter 13 explains how you can use your children to save tax. If you have to pay income tax on some of your interest income, one thing you can do is give money to your adult children so that they can earn tax-free interest. In one example this produces an overall saving of £2,340 after a few years.

## Part 5 Savings Platforms & Premium Bonds

Chapter 14 shows how, by using an online savings platform like Hargreaves Lansdown's Active Savings, you can effortlessly transfer your savings from bank to bank, thereby maximising your interest income.

Chapter 15 is all about premium bonds, which allow you to earn tax-free prizes of up to £1 million. An investment in premium bonds can be an attractive alternative to a taxed savings account if you're a higher-rate taxpayer or additional-rate taxpayer.

## Part 6 Sole Traders & Company Owners

In Chapter 16 we turn our focus to savings accounts available to sole traders and company owners. Why keep all your business cash in a current account when you can earn a decent amount of interest by opening an easy-access savings account? We also explain how company owners can get some of the company's cash into their own hands, so that they can earn tax-free interest.

Chapter 17 covers directors who *borrow* money from their companies and directors who *lend* money to their companies. A couple who run a company together can borrow up to £20,000 tax free for up to 21 months. Bigger loans can be made extremely cheaply.

And if you lend money to your company any interest the company pays to you could be both tax deductible for the company and tax free in your hands – the best case scenario when it comes to extracting cash from your company. Some company owners may be able to save over £1,000 by getting their companies to pay them interest.

## Part 7 Earn Tax-Free Interest by Paying Off Debt

Paying off your personal debt is a great way to earn tax-free interest. This is because paying less interest is just as good as earning it – and often better from a tax standpoint.

Chapter 18 looks at the benefits and drawbacks of paying down the mortgage on your home. Apart from earning tax-free interest, this may help you qualify for a better mortgage deal (by reducing the loan-to-value ratio on the property).

In Chapter 19 we compare paying down your mortgage with keeping money in a savings account. At present you may be able to enjoy a better tax-free return by keeping your money in a cash ISA... but paying off your mortgage may be more attractive than a taxed savings account.

Chapter 20 explains why paying off personal loans, credit cards and other short-term borrowings will often produce the highest returns of all. The average borrower will enjoy tax-free returns ranging from 9.05% to 22.45% per year.

In Chapters 21 and 22 we look at paying off buy-to-let mortgages and other business borrowings. As a general rule it's better to reduce your *personal* debt before you reduce your *business* debt – business debt enjoys tax relief and is therefore cheaper.

Landlords enjoy 20% tax relief on their interest payments and self-employed business owners who are higher-rate taxpayers enjoy 42% tax relief, sometimes as much as 62%.

However, sometimes these borrowers also face very high interest rates and loan arrangement fees. So these chapters show you how to quickly calculate the *after-tax* cost of your buy-to-let mortgages or other business borrowings.

Armed with this information you can decide whether it's worth using any spare cash you have to reduce these loans.

### *Company Owners with Business Premises*

Many company owners own their business premises *personally* and the company pays them rent. There may also be a mortgage on the property and the interest payments will enjoy full tax relief, making this one of the best types of debt to have. Many company owners who are higher-rate taxpayers will be enjoying 45% tax relief on their interest payments.

Chapter 23 shows you how to quickly calculate the after-tax cost of such a mortgage, so you can decide whether it's worth paying off early.

## Scope of this Guide

The aim of this guide is to help readers earn as much interest income as possible and, where possible, enjoy tax-free interest income.

The guide also looks at some of the benefits and drawbacks of using your savings to pay off various types of debt.

This subject is a big part of the world of money and finance. Hence I make no claim whatsoever that every angle is covered or covered in sufficient depth.

Furthermore, it's important to emphasize that everyone's personal financial situation is different. What may be appropriate for one person may not be appropriate for another.

For all of these reasons it's vital that you obtain professional advice before taking any action based on the information contained in this publication.

# Part 1

# Interest Rate Basics

# Chapter 1

# The Importance of
# <u>Real</u> Interest Rates

Savings accounts and similar investments currently pay more interest than they have for well over a decade.

For example, instead of earning 0.1% in an easy-access savings account, interest rates of around 5% are available from some banks nowadays.

Does this mean savings accounts and the like are good investments? Not necessarily because we also have to look at how *inflation* erodes the value of your savings.

The only reason savings rates have gone up is because the Bank of England has increased its 'base rate' 14 times since December 2021. And the reason the central bank has increased interest rates is to get a grip on runaway inflation.

Higher interest rates reduce demand in the economy: people with mortgages have less to spend on other things, savers are happy keeping their cash in the bank and businesses are more reluctant to make investments using borrowed money. Lower demand for goods and services makes it harder for shopkeepers, landlords and suppliers to raise their prices.

At least that's the theory. In reality inflation is a complex beast and the Bank of England can only do so much without wrecking the economy.

Interest rate increases also take a long time to work their way through the system, often well over a year.

Inflation peaked at around 11% in October 2022, the highest rate since 1981. At the time of writing it had fallen to 4% which is encouraging but still some way from the Bank of England's 2% target.

## Real versus Nominal Returns

To be a good or even acceptable long-term investment you have to be earning a *real* return on your savings.

In other words, your savings have to be rising in value faster than the prices of the goods and services you intend to buy with them.

For example, let's say you currently have £1,000 sitting in a savings account and use the money in 12 months' time to buy a variety of goods that currently cost £1,000.

If in a year's time your savings are worth £1,050 but the goods now cost £1,100 your savings will have lost some of their purchasing power. In other words, you will have become poorer. The *nominal* value of your savings may have risen but their *real* value has fallen.

For your savings to be rising in real terms the interest rate you are paid has to be higher than the inflation rate that is eroding them.

You can think of the real value of your savings as a bucket of water. Let's say the bucket is sitting underneath a slowly dripping tap. The dripping tap is the interest the bank pays you.

Let's also say the bucket has a small hole in the bottom which allows water to leak out. The hole is inflation.

If the water level in the bucket keeps rising, despite the hole in the bottom, this means your wealth is increasing in real terms, i.e. faster than inflation.

But if the water level is slowly falling, this means your wealth is falling in real terms – inflation is eroding their value faster than the bank is adding to them.

## Calculating the Real Return on Your Savings

The real return is calculated by subtracting the inflation rate from the nominal interest rate.

For example, if you're earning 5% and the inflation rate is 4% you'll be earning a positive real return of 1%:

$$\text{Nominal Interest Rate - Inflation Rate = Real Return}$$

$$5\% - 4\% = 1\%$$

A positive real return is what you want because it means your wealth is actually increasing – maybe not by much but still increasing nevertheless.

But if you are earning a nominal interest rate of 1.75% (what my own bank is paying on its easy-access savings account) and prices are rising by 4%, you'll be earning a negative real return of 2.25%.

$$1.75\% - 4\% = -2.25\%$$

A negative real return means your wealth is falling.

Although a negative real return of 2.25% means you're only getting a little bit poorer each year, over long periods of time the erosion of your wealth is significant. After 10 years your savings will have lost around 20% of their purchasing power.

(Note the formula employed above to calculate real interest rates is just an approximation, although it's the one most journalists and commentators use. At the end of this chapter we will take a closer look at the correct formula.)

## Real Returns and Tax

A major flaw in our tax system is you have to pay tax on nominal investment returns, not real returns. The Government forces you to pay tax on returns that are merely illusory.

For example, let's say you're earning 5% on your savings and have to pay 40% tax on this interest income. This means you'll be left with 3% after tax and your real return will fall to negative 1%:

$$3\% - 4\% \text{ inflation} = -1\%$$

After 10 years your savings will have lost around 10% of their purchasing power.

## Are Savings Accounts Good Investments?

Those who shop around can find savings accounts paying somewhere between 5% and 5.5% interest at present (the rates vary between easy-access accounts and fixed-term accounts).

That's more than the current inflation rate, which at the time of writing was 4%.

It is therefore possible to earn a small positive real return on your savings... if we ignore any income tax that is payable.

If you have to pay 40% or 45% income tax on your interest income inflation will slowly erode the real value of your savings, even if you're shopping around for the savings accounts that pay the most interest.

Those who do not shop around will probably be earning a negative real return both before and after tax.

However, it's important to point out that the much publicised inflation number is backward looking, showing how prices have risen in the *previous* 12 months.

If you put your money in a fixed-rate account paying 5.25% over the next 12 months and inflation averages 2.5% during this period, you will enjoy a positive real return, even if you have to pay income tax at 45% on your interest income.

Of course none of us can predict what will happen to inflation over the next 12 months and it is perhaps wishful thinking to expect it to fall to 2.5%. Nevertheless it is worth pointing out that it is the *expected* inflation rate that matters, not the historical one.

It's also important to point out that everybody's inflation rate is different. The number reported in the media each month is based on a basket of goods and services called the Consumer Price Index or CPI.

If the basket of goods and services that *you* buy is different to this basket, your personal inflation rate will be higher or lower.

Research has shown that high income households are less affected by rising food prices, rents and fuel costs (the main contributors to inflation in recent times) than poorer households.

If you are a high income earner it's possible your personal inflation rate will be at least one percentage point lower than the published rate. In other words, you may be earning a modest real return on your savings, even though most people aren't!

In summary:

- Those who shop around for the best interest rates are probably earning a small positive real return (before tax) on their savings.

- Those who have to pay income tax at 40% or 45% on their interest income will probably be earning a negative real return, unless inflation falls in the months ahead.

- Those who do not shop around are very likely suffering negative real returns both before and after tax.

Thus the best savings accounts and other interest-earning investments are arguably acceptable long-term investments if you are an extremely risk-averse investor and do not have to pay income tax on your interest income.

(For some individuals, especially retirees, capital preservation is more important than capital gains and capital preservation is one thing savings accounts offer in spades.)

If you have to pay income tax on your interest income, savings accounts and other interest-earning investments are arguably unattractive long-term investments because your wealth will be slowly eroded by inflation.

However, this does not mean you should avoid them.

Savings accounts and other similar investments are a great place to temporarily store cash you intend to invest elsewhere when conditions are favourable.

They are also a great place to store money you may need in the near future because, unlike almost every other investment you can make, the value of your savings generally cannot fall in nominal terms.

It's true the financial institution you entrust with your savings could go bankrupt. But there are safeguards in place such as the Financial Services Compensation Scheme, which protects £85,000 per person per banking group (see Chapter 2).

There are other interest-paying investments, like money market funds, that are a bit more risky (see Chapter 9). However, they are still extremely low-risk investments – much less risky than investing in equities or property.

Although savings accounts may not be viable long-term investments for many individuals, I have enormous sympathy for anyone who keeps all their money in the bank.

Those of us who have experience investing in the stock market know just how gut wrenching it is to watch share prices fall by 50% or more during a market crash. Investing is difficult!

If you do keep a significant amount of your wealth in savings accounts and similar investments it's important to:

- **Shop around for the best interest rates**. This wasn't as important a few years ago when almost all banks were paying paltry amounts of interest. There's a good chance the bank you use for your day to day banking is paying uncompetitive interest on savings. This is especially the case with easy-access savings accounts. As I pointed out earlier, my own bank is currently paying 1.75%, although rates of 5% or more are available elsewhere.

- **Earn tax-free interest** so that your savings have the best possible chance of keeping pace with inflation. Earning tax-free interest is what this guide is all about.

## The Correct Way to Calculate Real Returns

Earlier in this chapter I stated that the real return on your savings is calculated as follows:

Real Return = Nominal Interest Rate *minus* Inflation Rate

For example, if you're earning 5% and inflation is 3% your real return is 2%.

However, as it turns out, the above equation is just an approximation.

The correct formula is called the "Fisher equation" (after the American economist Irving Fisher) and looks like this:

$$\textbf{Real Interest Rate} = \left[ \frac{1 + \text{Nominal Interest Rate}}{1 + \text{Inflation Rate}} \right] - 1$$

Note the inflation rate in the above equation is the *expected* inflation rate, not the rate reported in the papers which is backward looking.

For example, let's say you can earn 5% from a one-year fixed deposit and expect inflation to be 3% over the next year. Your real return will be 1.94%:

$$\textbf{Real Interest Rate} = \left[ \frac{1 + 0.05}{1 + 0.03} \right] - 1 = 1.94\%$$

Note we express percentages as fractions by dividing by 100. So 5% is expressed as 5/100 which is 0.05.

1.94% is very close to 2% and the approximation is perfectly acceptable in most cases.

However, I always think it's good to know how to do things correctly. Most financial journalists and financial advisors have never heard of the Fisher equation, even though earning real returns (beating inflation) is the number one goal of every investor.

Most people also think the approximation makes more sense intuitively than the Fisher equation. If your savings increase by 10% and prices rise 5%, surely you have made a real return of 5%?

The following example illustrates why the result we get from the Fisher equation – 4.76% – does actually make more sense:

### *Example*
*Buffy has £100 sitting in her bank account and uses all her money to buy a good which currently costs £1. This means she can currently buy 100 units of the good.*

*Alternatively she can leave her money in the bank and buy the good in a year's time. Let's assume she will earn 10% interest and the price of the good will rise by 5%.*

*In a year's time she will have £110 in the bank and the good will cost £1.05p. This means she can now afford 104.76 units of the good (£110/£1.05p) instead of 100.*

*The number of units she can afford has increased by 4.76%. This means her wealth has increased by 4.76% in real terms (and not by 5%).*

# Chapter 2

# The Financial Services Compensation Scheme

Financial Services Compensation Scheme (FSCS) protection is available to those who hold accounts with UK authorised banks, building societies and credit unions.

UK authorised means authorised by the Prudential Regulation Authority.

You will often see the 'FSCS Protected' logo on UK banks' websites.

In the event of a bank failure, the FSCS will automatically pay you back your money within 7 to 10 days up to a maximum of £85,000 per person per banking group.

What this means is that, if you hold multiple accounts with the same bank, a total of £85,000 will be protected. For example, if you hold £50,000 in a current account and £50,000 in a savings account with the same bank, £85,000 will be protected and £15,000 will be at risk.

But if you have 10 accounts at 10 different banks and each account holds £85,000, the whole £850,000 will be protected.

Those who hold large amounts of cash are therefore encouraged to spread their money across multiple banks to enjoy full protection.

## Banking Groups

The £85,000 limit applies per banking licence.

In most cases the banks are completely separate entities and you can enjoy £85,000 protection per bank.

However, some banks share a licence which could limit the amount of compensation you would receive.

For example, Bank of Scotland, Bank of Wales, Birmingham Midshires and Halifax are part of the same banking group and share one banking licence.

So if you have £100,000 deposited across all of these banks a total of just £85,000 will be protected.

HSBC and First Direct also share a banking licence.

The FSCS has a useful tool on its website that lets you check your protection levels by adding your various accounts at different banks:

www.fscs.org.uk/check/check-your-money-is-protected

## Making the Most of High Interest Rates

FSCS protection allows you to shop around and deposit your money in the bank that offers the highest interest rate.

Personally, I have never heard of some of the banks that offer the best deals on price comparison websites or savings platforms like Hargreaves Lansdown's Active Savings (see Chapter 14).

Without FSCS protection, I would never deposit a single penny in any of these banks. But with FSCS protection I am happy to place my savings in whichever bank offers the highest interest rate.

Those with cash balances of more than £85,000 face a more difficult trade off.

If you have to spread your money across more than one bank to enjoy FSCS protection you will inevitably earn less interest – the first £85,000 can go to the bank paying the most interest, the rest will have to go to the second-best bank and maybe also the third-best bank ...and so on.

Another reason why you may earn less interest by spreading your savings around is that banks often reward bigger depositors with higher interest rates. As an example, RBS pays instant access account holders with more than £250,000 1.05% more interest than those who have just £85,000 in their accounts.

## Joint Accounts

Couples often have joint accounts. With joint accounts *each person* enjoys up to £85,000 protection per banking group, so up to £170,000 in total.

For example, if you and your spouse have a joint account holding £100,000, the entire amount will be protected (£50,000 each). This means you could each hold an additional £35,000 in other accounts at the same banking group and enjoy full protection.

## Business Accounts

Business accounts are also protected by the Financial Services Compensation Scheme. (Most businesses are protected but certain financial services firms are not.)

The protection is different for sole traders and companies.

A sole trader business does not enjoy a separate legal identity – the owner and the business are treated as one and the same.

Thus if a sole trader holds personal and business accounts with the same bank, the FSCS will protect up to £85,000 in total.

If you have £30,000 in your personal account and £100,000 in your business account, a total of £85,000 will be protected and £45,000 will be at risk.

Companies, on the other hand, are separate legal entities and enjoy their own protection up to £85,000 per banking group.

Thus if you and your company have accounts at the same bank, you will enjoy up to £85,000 of protection personally and your company will enjoy up to £85,000 of protection.

For example, if you have £20,000 in your personal account and £200,000 in your company account, the £20,000 in your personal account will be protected and £85,000 of the company's cash will be protected, leaving £115,000 at risk.

Companies with large cash balances in excess of £85,000 should consider spreading their money across more than one bank.

## Cash Held in SIPPs and Stocks & Shares ISAs

If you have a self-invested personal pension (SIPP) or stocks and shares ISA, a significant amount of your pension or ISA savings may be held in cash at any one time.

Investment platforms like AJ Bell and Hargreaves Lansdown will typically take your cash and spread it across a number of banks and then pay you interest.

For example, AJ Bell says it holds customer cash with up to 14 banks.

If one of those banks fails your cash held with that bank will be covered by the FSCS, up to the £85,000 limit.

Note, however, that if you also hold a personal account with that failed bank the £85,000 limit applies to both the cash held in your personal account and your SIPP or ISA cash.

For example, let's say you have £75,000 in a personals savings account with Bank X and £250,000 cash in your SIPP, £25,000 of which is held with Bank X.

Your total exposure to Bank X is £100,000 so if it fails £15,000 of your cash will be at risk (£100,000 less £85,000 FSCS protection).

## Debts versus Savings

What happens if you have both savings and borrowings with a bank that fails?

The FSCS will not deduct your debts from your savings. Compensation is paid on what they call a "gross basis".

So if you have £20,000 in a savings account and £5,000 of credit card debt you will still be paid £20,000.

Your £5,000 credit card debt will not be written off and will still have to be repaid (for example, the failed bank's loan book could be sold to another firm).

What if you have more than £85,000 of savings in a bank that fails but also have a loan with the same bank?

For example, let's say you have £100,000 in a savings account and a mortgage balance of £200,000.

You will be entitled to compensation of just £85,000 from the FSCS but, under insolvency law, your remaining deposit balance of £15,000 will be deducted from your £200,000 mortgage balance.

## Temporary High Balances

In certain circumstances you are entitled to compensation of more than £85,000 when a bank fails.

The FSCS protects "temporary high balances" that result from "major life events".

An additional £1 million can be protected for up to six months.

The £1 million limit applies per person, per life event, per banking group.

Major life events include:

- Main residence purchases
- Main residence sales
- Inheritances
- Insurance payouts
- Redundancy payments
- Retirement benefits
- Divorce settlements
- Unfair dismissals

Personal injury compensation enjoys unlimited protection (i.e. more than £1 million).

In addition you can also benefit from the usual £85,000 of normal protection for your regular savings.

Note, if you sell a buy-to-let property or second home this will not be protected by the temporary high balance rules – only main residences are covered.

House sales and purchases are treated as separate life events. For example, if you sell your house before buying a new one, the house purchase will start a fresh six-month period of protection.

Note a claim under the temporary high balance rules is not as straightforward as the ordinary automatic payouts of up to £85,000.

The FSCS would need to review all the available evidence to satisfy itself that there is indeed a connection between the relevant life event and the money in your bank account.

In other words, it's a bit of a grey area and it is probably still advisable, where possible, to spread high balances across several banking groups.

## Living Abroad

You don't have to live in the UK to enjoy protection, as long as your bank is UK authorised.

# Chapter 3

# The Importance of Annual Equivalent Rates

When comparing bank account interest rates you'll often see two rates quoted: the gross rate and the annual equivalent rate (AER).

For example, you may see an advertised gross rate of 4.6% with an AER of 4.7%.

Gross simply means the stated interest rate before any income tax is deducted. In the past banks deducted 20% tax from customers' interest payments and paid it to HMRC. This is no longer required and all stated interest rates are effectively gross interest rates.

The annual equivalent rate is more useful for comparing savings accounts because it lets you see how much interest you will earn over a year, taking into account how often interest is added to your account balance and compounded, allowing you to earn interest on interest.

With many savings accounts interest is calculated daily and then paid into your account monthly. With other accounts interest may also be calculated daily but only paid into your account quarterly or once a year.

The more often interest is paid out and compounded the better.

An account paying interest once a year may have a higher stated interest rate than an account paying interest monthly. However, when interest is compounded the account paying interest monthly may give you a better return.

The annual equivalent rate takes account of these differences and makes it easier to compare different offers.

In summary, it's the AER you should look at when comparing savings products and you should always see this information clearly stated.

## Calculating the Annual Equivalent Rate

The formula is:

$$AER = (1 + i/n)^n - 1$$

**i** is the stated gross interest rate
**n** is the number of times a year interest is paid (compounded)

For example, let's say a bank is advertising a gross rate of 4.6%. Interest is calculated daily and added to your account monthly. The AER is 4.7%, calculated as follows:

$$AER = (1 + 0.046/12)^{12} - 1 = 0.04698$$

Remember we express percentages as fractions by dividing by 100. So 4.6% is expressed as 4.6/100 which is 0.046.

The AER is 4.698% which rounds up to 4.7%.

What the AER means in practice is that if you place £1,000 in a bank account with a gross interest rate of 4.6% paid monthly you will earn £46.98 interest over 12 months and your balance will be £1,046.98 at the end of the year.

If interest is only paid out quarterly the AER will be 4.68%, calculated by replacing "n" in the above formula with 4.

If interest is compounded more than once a year the annual equivalent rate will always be higher than the stated gross interest rate.


## Interest Paid Less Frequently

With a few fixed-rate bonds lasting more than a year the interest is only paid out on maturity, for example after two years or even after five years.

In this case the AER will be *lower* than the stated gross interest rate.

For example, if you're offered a five-year fixed rate bond with a stated gross interest rate of 3.75% and interest paid on maturity, the AER will be 3.5%. (This is calculated by replacing "n" in the above formula with 0.2)

By contrast, a five-year fixed rate bond with a stated gross interest rate of 3.85% and interest paid annually will have an AER of 3.85%.

Clearly 3.85% is a lot better than 3.5%.

## Comparing Savings Accounts

With most easy-access savings accounts interest is paid monthly and so the annual equivalent rate will be higher than the stated gross interest rate.

However, the important thing to remember about easy-access accounts is the interest rate is *variable* and can be reduced at any time.

Thus if you are currently earning an annual equivalent rate of 4.7% this may not in fact last a whole year. (Of course, interest rates can also increase but most commentators think the future direction is down.)

With many fixed-rate bonds lasting one to five years interest is paid once a year so the AER and gross interest rate are the same. (We replace "n" in the above formula with 1.)

For example, at the time of writing you can earn a gross interest rate of 4.6% for three years with interest paid annually. Because interest is paid once a year the AER is also 4.6%.

You could also earn 4.6% from an easy-access account with interest paid monthly and an AER of 4.7%.

Thus at present you can obtain a higher annual equivalent rate from an easy-access account, while at the same time retaining full access to your savings. By contrast, with most fixed-rate bonds, you cannot get your hands on your money until the product matures.

However, this does not mean the easy-access account will deliver more interest over the whole investment period. Because interest rates on easy-access accounts can be reduced, it's possible you will earn much less than 4.7% per year if you keep your savings in the easy-access account for three years.

At present many fixed-rate bonds pay less interest to those who are prepared to tie up their money for longer. For example, you may be able to obtain an interest rate of 4.85% from a one-year fix but just 4.6% per year from a three-year fix.

Normally you would expect to be rewarded for tying up your savings for longer, so one can only assume the banks expect interest rates to fall in the future.

In conclusion, the annual equivalent rate is useful for comparing bank accounts of the *same type*, for example easy-access accounts offered by different banks or one-year fixed-rate bonds offered by different banks.

However, it is less useful for comparing different types of account, for example easy-access accounts and fixed-rate bonds.

# Part 2

# How Interest Income Is Taxed

# Chapter 4

# The Personal Savings Allowance & Starting Rate Band

If your cash savings are held inside an ISA or pension there is no income tax payable on your interest income.

Interest income earned outside these tax wrappers may also be tax free thanks to the:

- £5,000 starting-rate band
- £1,000/£500 personal savings allowance

Your interest income may also be tax free if you have a very low level of income overall which is all covered by your £12,570 income tax personal allowance.

Although most individuals can shelter all of their interest income from tax by putting their money in a cash ISA, the personal savings allowance and starting rate band may give you the freedom to put your savings in an account that pays the most competitive interest rate, which may not be a cash ISA.

They may also free up more of your annual ISA allowance to invest in the stock market, if that's what you prefer to do.

If you receive a large cash lump sum you may also struggle to shelter the money in an ISA because you can only invest £20,000 per tax year.

For example, if you sell your home or receive a big dividend from your company it may not be possible to put all the money into an ISA in a single tax year.

The personal savings allowance and starting-rate band may help out in these situations.

Other types of interest income can never be sheltered inside an ISA, for example:

- When you lend money to a friend or family member
- When you lend money to your own company

Once again the personal savings allowance and starting-rate band may help out in these circumstances.

## The £5,000 Starting-Rate Band

The starting-rate band provides a 0% tax rate for up to £5,000 of interest income, however in most cases only those on low incomes can use it.

This is because the £5,000 starting-rate band is reduced by any *non-savings income* you have in excess of the £12,570 personal allowance. Non-savings income includes:

- Employment income
- Self-employment income
- Pension income
- Rental income

Hence, if your non-savings income exceeds £17,570 in total (£12,570 + £5,000), none of your interest income will be covered by the starting rate band.

Of course, most regular salary earners and self-employed business owners will have more than £17,570 of non-savings income. Many company owners are in a different position, however. Note that the above list of non-savings income does NOT include dividends. Dividends are treated as the top slice of your income and do not use up the starting-rate band.

Because many company owners pay themselves a salary of no more than £12,570 and take the rest of their income as dividends, they will often have little or no taxable non-savings income. As a result, many can earn at least £5,000 of tax-free interest.

We'll take a closer look at company owners in Chapter 7.

Others who can use the 0% starting rate include spouses who don't work (or work part time) and retirees with modest pensions.

### Example
*Denise has a salary of £20,000 and interest income of £2,000. The first £12,570 of her salary is tax free and the remaining £7,430 is taxed at 20%. This £7,430 of taxable non-savings income effectively "eats up" her £5,000 starting-rate band. She is, however, entitled to a £1,000 personal savings allowance (discussed below) which shelters £1,000 of her interest income from tax. The remaining £1,000 of her interest income will be taxed at 20%.*

### Example
*Fiona's husband earns a substantial salary so she decides to stop working for a few years to raise their children and save on childcare costs. The couple have a rental property which they place in her name, as well as savings that produce taxable interest.*

*She earns rental income of £14,400 and interest income of £3,000. The first £12,570 of her rental income is tax free and the remaining £1,830 is taxed at 20%. This £1,830 of taxable non-savings income leaves her with a starting-rate band of £3,170 (£5,000 - £1,830). This means all of her £3,000 interest income is tax free.*

### Example
*The facts are the same as before except Fiona also has £10,000 of dividend income from a share portfolio held outside an ISA. Her dividends are the top slice of her income and do not use up any of her starting-rate band. Thus all of her interest income will continue to be tax free.*

## Personal Savings Allowance

The personal savings allowance lets you earn the following amounts of tax-free interest:

- £1,000  Basic-rate taxpayers (income up to £50,270)
- £500  Higher-rate taxpayers (income over £50,270)
- £0  Additional-rate taxpayers (income over £125,140)

The personal savings allowance is much less valuable today than it was a few years ago. The allowance has been frozen at £1,000 (basic-rate taxpayers) and £500 (higher-rate taxpayers) since it was introduced in April 2016.

The £1,000 allowance should be around £1,450 today to compensate for inflation and the £500 allowance should be around £725.

Furthermore, interest rates have increased significantly since the Bank of England started raising them in December 2021. Back then it wasn't unusual to earn 0.1% in an easy-access savings account.

Nowadays you could be earning around 5% from one of these accounts and interest rates of over 5% are available to those willing to tie up their savings for a year or more.

The end result is many more savers are earning interest in excess of the personal savings allowance and are thus having to pay income tax on their interest income.

For example, a higher-rate taxpayer with around £10,000 of savings could easily be earning more than £500 of interest income and paying income tax on the excess.

It's also important to mention the Government's Big Freeze of tax thresholds.

The £50,270 higher-rate threshold has been frozen for seven years until April 2028. As a result more and more people are becoming higher-rate taxpayers and paying 40% tax, even though their income has not increased in real terms.

To add insult to injury they are also seeing their personal savings allowance reduced from £1,000 to just £500.

Similarly, the additional-rate threshold was reduced from £150,000 to £125,140 on 6th April 2023. As a result, significantly more people now have to pay the 45% top rate of tax.

Furthermore, additional-rate taxpayers are not entitled to any personal savings allowance and generally have to pay income tax on ALL their interest income, unless their savings are sheltered inside an ISA or pension.

### Personal Savings Allowance Calculations

The personal savings allowance operates separately from, and in addition to, the starting-rate band. This means some individuals can earn up to £6,000 of tax-free interest every year.

Income that falls within your savings allowance still uses up your basic-rate band or higher-rate band.

It may therefore affect the level of savings allowance you're entitled to and the rate of tax payable on any interest income you receive in excess of the allowance.

### Example
*Alan has a salary of £50,000 and interest income of £250 – total income £50,250.*

*This is just below the £50,270 higher-rate threshold so he'll be entitled to a £1,000 personal savings allowance and all of his interest income will be tax free.*

### Example
*Gudrun has salary and rental income of £49,400 and interest income of £1,000 – total income £50,400.*

*As a higher-rate taxpayer she is only entitled to a £500 personal savings allowance. Thus £500 of her interest income will be tax free and this will use up £500 of her basic-rate band, leaving £370 taxed at 20%. The final £130 falls over the £50,270 higher-rate threshold and will be taxed at 40%.*

# Chapter 5

# The Tax Rates on Interest Income

Once the various tax-free allowances have been used up your interest income is taxed at the 'normal' income tax rates namely:

- 20%   Income between £12,570 and £50,270
- 40%   Income between £50,270 and £100,000
- 60%   Income between £100,000 and £125,140
- 45%   Income over £125,140

In the examples that follow we will assume that the £5,000 starting-rate band is not available because the taxpayer's income is too high to qualify (as explained in the previous chapter).

We will also assume that the interest income is not sheltered in an ISA (perhaps because the individual is already making full use of his or her ISA allowance).

## Basic-Rate Taxpayers

Basic-rate taxpayers enjoy a personal savings allowance of £1,000 and any additional interest income is taxed at 20%.

### *Example*
*Cara earns a salary of £40,000 and interest income of £2,000. She has no other income. As a basic-rate taxpayer the first £1,000 of her interest income is tax free thanks to her personal savings allowance. The remaining £1,000 is taxed at 20%.*

Cara is a bit unusual because most basic-rate taxpayers will be able to completely avoid paying income tax on their interest income.

This is because most will be able to shelter all their interest income from tax in an ISA (most basic-rate taxpayers will not be earning enough income to max out their £20,000 annual ISA allowance).

There are exceptions of course. Some will have high-income partners who can gift them £20,000 each year so that their ISA allowance is fully utilised.

Any additional savings will then generate interest income that is potentially taxable.

However, with a personal savings allowance of £1,000 basic-rate taxpayers can currently hold around £20,000 in a savings account (not an ISA) earning 5% interest tax free.

Any additional interest income will then be taxed at 20%.

If you pay 20% tax on any of your interest income the after-tax return on those savings can be calculated by multiplying the interest rate by 0.8.

For example if you are earning 5% on your taxed savings your after-tax return will be:

$$5\% \times 0.8 = 4\%$$

This is an important calculation because you can compare your after-tax interest rate with the inflation rate to determine whether you are earning a real return on your savings (see Chapter 1).

At the time of writing the inflation rate was 4% so a taxpayer in this situation would be getting neither richer nor poorer.

## Higher-Rate Taxpayers

Higher-rate taxpayers enjoy a personal savings allowance of £500 and any additional interest income is taxed at 40%.

### Example
*Nikki earns a salary of £80,000 and interest income of £1,500. She has no other income. As a higher-rate taxpayer the first £500 of her interest income is tax free thanks to her personal savings allowance. The remaining £1,000 is taxed at 40%.*

Higher-rate taxpayers can currently keep up to £10,000 in a savings account earning 5% interest tax free. Any additional interest income will then be taxed at 40%.

If you pay 40% tax on any of your interest income the after-tax return on those savings can be calculated by multiplying the interest rate by 0.6.

For example, if you are earning 5% on your taxed savings your after-tax return is:

$$5\% \times 0.6 = 3\%$$

This is less than the current inflation rate, which means you would be earning a negative real return on your savings (i.e. getting poorer).

Taxpayers who have to pay 40% income tax on some of their interest income should consider gifting cash to their spouse or partner if that person can earn tax-free interest or pay tax at just 20%.

Beyond keeping a healthy cash reserve to meet any unforeseen expenses they could also consider using their surplus savings to invest in other assets that may beat inflation or perhaps to make pension contributions (see Chapter 12).


## Personal Allowance Withdrawal

If your income goes over the £100,000 threshold your income tax personal allowance is gradually withdrawn. Once your income reaches £125,140 you will have no personal allowance left.

The combination of 40% tax and having your personal allowance withdrawn produces a marginal income tax rate of 60%.

People in this income bracket are still higher-rate taxpayers and enjoy a £500 personal savings allowance.

### Example
*Steven earns a salary of £100,000 and interest income of £5,000. He has no other income. The first £500 of his interest income is tax free thanks to his personal savings allowance. The remaining £4,500 is taxed at 60%.*

Those in the £100,000-£125,140 income bracket will enjoy a very low after-tax return on their taxed interest income. For example, if you are earning 5% on your taxed savings your after-tax return is:

$$5\% \times 0.4 = 2\%$$

Once again taxpayers who find themselves paying 60% tax on some of their interest income should consider gifting surplus cash to their spouse or partner, if that person will be able to earn tax-free interest or pay tax at just 40% or 20%.

They should also consider alternative investments and pension contributions.

## Additional-Rate Taxpayers

Additional-rate taxpayers (income over £125,140) do not enjoy any personal savings allowance and typically pay 45% on ALL their interest income.

If you are earning 5% on your savings your after-tax return will be:

$$5\% \times 0.55 = 2.75\%$$

This is less than the current 4% inflation rate.

Once again surplus cash should perhaps be gifted, invested somewhere else or used to make pension contributions.

## Scottish Taxpayers

If you live in Scotland you probably know that different income tax rates apply to most types of income such as salaries, rental income and profits from self employment. Most notably, once you earn more than £43,662 you become a higher-rate taxpayer and start paying income tax at 42%.

However, the Scottish income tax rates do NOT apply to interest income and dividends.

For example, let's say you're a Scottish taxpayer with a £45,000 salary and £2,500 of interest income. You may be a Scottish higher-rate taxpayer when it comes to your salary but you're still a UK basic-rate taxpayer with respect to your interest income.

As a result the first £1,000 of your interest income will be tax free thanks to the personal savings allowance and the remaining £1,500 will be taxed at just 20%.

If you have a salary of £60,000 and £2,500 of interest income you will be a higher-rate taxpayer in both Scotland and the rest of the UK.

## How Is Income Tax Collected?

When the personal savings allowance was introduced the automatic deduction of 20% income tax by banks and building societies and other financial institutions ceased.

Any tax due on interest income is generally collected through the PAYE system (through adjustments to your tax code) or when you submit your tax return.

However, your current tax code may be based on old information supplied by the banks and building societies. The actual interest you earn during the current tax year may be significantly higher or lower than what you earned last year (for example, if you've made significant deposits or withdrawals).

For this reason it's important to keep a close eye on your tax code and let HMRC know if any changes are required.

# Chapter 6

# <u>When</u> Interest Income Is Taxed

The income tax legislation states that income tax is payable "on the full amount of the interest arising in the tax year".

When does interest arise?

According to HMRC, interest arises when it is received or made available. Interest has been made available "if it is credited to an account on which the account holder is free to draw".

With most easy-access savings accounts interest is calculated daily and added to your account once a month. When it is credited to your account you are free to withdraw it.

The interest will therefore be taxable in the tax year in which it is credited to your account.

## Fixed-Rate Savings Accounts

Savers can also put their money in fixed-rate savings accounts (also known as savings bonds) which guarantee a set interest rate for a specified period – anything from one month to five years.

With these accounts interest is typically calculated daily but may only be credited to your account once a year (or on maturity if the bond is for 12 months or less).

With some fixed-rate accounts interest is credited to your account monthly. This is better because it means you will earn interest on your interest.

What is the income tax position?

It doesn't matter when the interest is credited to your account, what matters is when you can access the interest.

Interest becomes taxable at the point you can access it.

Whether the interest is credited to your account monthly or annually, if you can only access it when the savings bond matures, the interest will only be taxed in the tax year in which the product matures.

Many fixed-rate savings products do not give you access to either your interest or initial capital until the end of the period.

For example, with Zopa's fixed term savings accounts interest is calculated daily and paid into your account monthly. However, the bank states that "all of your money, including interest, is only accessible at the end of the term".

According to Zopa: "You only need to consider tax on your earnings in the financial year the fixed term ends."

With products such as these, where your interest income cannot be withdrawn, income tax is only payable at the end of the term, which could be anything up to five years.

### Example
*Denise invests £10,000 in Zopa's five year fixed term savings account. The gross interest rate is currently 4.21% but because interest is credited monthly, the annual equivalent rate is 4.3% (see Chapter 3).*

*She earns £430 interest in year 1, £448 in year 2, £468 in year 3, £488 in year 4 and £509 in year 5. The amount goes up each year thanks to compounding (she earns interest on previous years' interest).*

*After five years she will have accumulated £2,343 of interest income and this will all be taxable in the tax year the product matures.*

*If Denise is a higher-rate taxpayer the first £500 will be tax free thanks to her personal savings allowance and the remaining £1,843 will be taxed at 40%, resulting in a tax bill of £737.*

If Denise was earning the same return from an easy-access account or a fixed-rate account that gave her access to her interest income, almost all her interest income would be tax free.

This is because she would have less than £500 of taxable interest every year (except year 5), and this would all be covered by her personal savings allowance.

Only in year 5 does she earn more than £500 interest which would result in a tax bill of just £4 (£9 x 40%).

Some savers should therefore think carefully about going for long-term fixed-rate savings accounts where all the interest income is taxed in a single tax year and exceeds their personal savings allowance.

## Fixed Rate Accounts with Access

Some fixed-rate savings products may allow you to have your interest paid out. Or you may be allowed access to your money if you're prepared to pay a penalty for early access.

According to HMRC, since you are allowed to draw on the funds, even though with a penalty, the interest is taxable in the tax year it is credited to your savings account.

If the terms and conditions of the savings product do not allow you to withdraw or have access to your interest when it is credited to your account, and you have to wait until the maturity date, the interest will only arise and be taxed at that point.

## When Paying Tax at the End May Be Better

In some cases having all your interest income taxed in a single year will not increase your tax bill.

This would be the case if you have other savings and the interest on those other savings already uses up your personal savings allowance.

Paying tax at 20% or 40% in the final year will not be more costly than paying tax at 20% or 40% every year.

An exception would be where you earn a big chunk of interest in a single tax year and this pushes you into a higher tax bracket.

For example, if you normally have total income of less than £50,270 but a big interest receipt pushes you over the higher-rate threshold, your personal savings allowance will be reduced from £1,000 to £500 *and* you will pay 40% instead of 20% on the excess.

If you normally have total income of less than £100,000 but a big interest receipt pushes you over this threshold, you will pay 60% tax instead of 40% on some of your interest income.

If you are an additional-rate taxpayer (income over £125,140) you aren't entitled to any personal savings allowance, so having all your interest income taxed at 45% in the final year will probably not increase your overall tax bill.

For some taxpayers paying income tax in a single tax year may, in fact, result in a *lower* tax bill. This is because rolling up interest tax free can be better than paying tax every year.

### *Example*
*Glynn is a higher-rate taxpayer and has other savings that already use up his £500 personal savings allowance. Thus he will pay 40% tax on any additional interest income he earns.*

*He has an additional £10,000 to invest for five years and is trying to choose between two accounts: one which gives him access to his interest income as it is credited to his account and another that only gives him access after five years. Both accounts pay 4.3% interest for five years.*

*With the account that only allows access after five years he will receive £2,343 interest in year 5 and pay 40% tax, leaving him with £1,406.*

*With the account that allows him to access his interest he will have to pay 40% tax every year, leaving him with less after-tax interest to compound.*

*For example, in year 1 he will receive £430 interest, pay 40% tax, leaving him with an additional amount of just £258 on which to earn interest over the next four years. In year 2 he will receive £441 interest, pay 40% tax, leaving him with an additional amount of just £265 on which he earn interest over the next three years.*

*After five years his account will have earned £1,358 of after-tax interest, compared with £1,406 if his interest was able to roll up without tax deducted every year.*

Paying income tax in a single tax year may provide significant additional tax savings if you expect to be in a *lower* tax bracket in the future:

### *Example*
*Rae is an additional-rate taxpayer (income over £125,140). In five year's time she expects to retire and become a basic-rate taxpayer (income under £50,270).*

*She has a total of £20,000 in savings. If she invests in an account paying 4.3%, and which allows her to access her interest income, she will pay 45% tax every year. After five years she will have received £2,480 of after-tax interest.*

*If she invests in a five-year savings bond, also paying 4.3% but with no access to her interest until maturity, she will receive £4,686 interest in year five. The first £1,000 will be tax free thanks to her personal savings allowance and the remaining interest will be taxed at 20%. After tax she will be left with £3,949.*

*In summary, if she pays tax in year five, when she becomes a basic-rate taxpayer, she will be left with £1,469 more after-tax interest.*

# Chapter 7

# Company Owners with Interest Income

Many company owners can earn £5,000 of tax-free interest each year thanks to the 0% starting-rate band.

The starting rate is supposed to benefit those with low incomes. Hence the £5,000 starting rate band is reduced by any *non-savings* income you have in excess of your personal allowance, including:

- Employment income
- Self-employment income
- Pension income
- Rental income

Hence, if your non-savings income exceeds £17,570 in total (£12,570 + £5,000), none of your interest income will be covered by the starting-rate band.

Of course, most regular salary earners and self-employed business owners will have more than £17,570 of non-savings income. Many company owners are in a different position, however. Note that the above list of non-savings income does NOT include dividends. Dividends are treated as the top slice of income and do not use up the starting-rate band.

Because many company owners often pay themselves a salary of no more than £12,750 (free from income tax and employee's national insurance) and take the rest of their income as dividends, they will often have little or no taxable non-savings income. As a result, some can earn at least £5,000 of tax-free interest.

### *Example*
*Mandy is a company owner with a salary of £12,570, dividend income of £30,000 and interest income of £5,000. Her salary is free from income tax thanks to her personal allowance and she therefore has no taxable non-savings income that uses up her starting-rate band (her dividend income does not count). Her interest income is fully covered by her £5,000 starting-rate band and taxed at 0%.*

Thanks to the starting-rate band some company owners will therefore pay 0% tax on their interest income if they:

- Take a small salary from their company,
- Do not have another source of employment income,
- Do not have a sole trader or partnership business,
- Don't earn much, if any, rental income, and
- Do not receive much, if any, pension income.

### *Example*
*The facts are exactly the same except Mandy also has rental income of £15,000. Her £15,000 of taxable non-savings income uses up all of her £5,000 starting-rate band, so none of her interest income will be tax free thanks to the 0% starting rate.*

*Her total taxable is £62,570. As a higher-rate taxpayer she is entitled to a £500 personal savings allowance which means £500 of her interest income is tax free. The remaining £4,500 is subject to income tax.*

It's important to point out that the 0% starting rate band is not given in addition to your basic-rate band (currently £37,700). Instead it is part of your basic-rate band.

If you qualify to use the starting-rate band your basic-rate band will be reduced, possibly pushing some of your dividend income into a higher tax bracket. We'll illustrate how this could affect your tax bill shortly.

## The Personal Savings Allowance

As we know from Chapter 4, the personal savings allowance exempts the first £1,000 of your interest income from tax if you're a basic-rate taxpayer and the first £500 if you're a higher-rate taxpayer. Additional-rate taxpayers don't qualify.

The personal savings allowance operates separately from, and in addition to, the starting-rate band. This means some company owners who are basic-rate taxpayers can earn up to £6,000 of tax-free interest every year and some higher-rate taxpayers can earn up to £5,500.

The personal savings allowance is helpful to company owners who cannot use the starting-rate band because they have too much non-savings income such as rental income. Most can still enjoy £1,000 or £500 of tax-free interest.

## Interest Income - Examples

### *Example – Basic-rate Taxpayer*

*Samantha is a company owner with a salary of £12,570 and interest income of £5,000. She also has £10,000 of rental income.*

*Her salary is covered by her personal allowance but thanks to her rental income she has £10,000 of taxable non-savings income. Because her taxable non-savings income exceeds the £5,000 starting rate limit, none of her interest income is covered by the 0% starting rate.*

*However, because she is a basic-rate taxpayer (her total income is less than £50,270) she is entitled to a £1,000 personal savings allowance. So £1,000 of her interest income will be tax free, the remaining £4,000 will be taxed at 20%.*

### *Example – Basic-rate Taxpayer*

*Janet is a company owner with a salary of £9,100, rental income of £7,500, interest income of £1,500 and dividends of £20,000 (total income £38,100).*

*There is no income tax on her salary and the first £3,470 of her rental income is covered by her remaining personal allowance. The final £4,030 of her rental income is taxed at 20% and uses up £4,030 of her £5,000 starting-rate band. Thus £970 of her interest income is covered by her remaining starting-rate band and is tax free.*

*As a basic-rate taxpayer she is also entitled to a £1,000 personal savings allowance, so the final £530 of her interest is also tax free.*

*In 2024/25 the first £500 of her dividend income is tax free thanks to the dividend allowance; the remaining £19,500 is taxed at 8.75%.*

(If you're wondering why Janet pays herself a salary of £9,100 instead of £12,570, this is often optimal when a director has income from other sources. £9,100 is the amount of salary that can be paid exempt from employer's national insurance. See the Taxcafe guide *Salary versus Dividends* for further information.)

### Example – Higher-rate Taxpayer

*Ollie is a company owner with a salary of £12,570 and dividends of £37,700. He also has interest income of £5,500 (total income £55,770).*

*There is no income tax on his salary and £5,000 of his interest income is tax free thanks to the 0% starting-rate band (dividends do not count as non-savings income and do not use up his starting-rate band).*

*Because his total income is £55,770 he is a higher-rate taxpayer and is entitled to a £500 personal savings allowance, so the final £500 of his interest income will also be tax free.*

*Turning to his dividend income, Ollie has £32,200 of his basic-rate band remaining (£50,270 - £12,570 - £5,500). Of this £500 will be tax free thanks to the dividend allowance and £31,700 will be taxed at 8.75%. The final £5,500 of his dividend income is taxed at 33.75%.*

*Although all of Ollie's interest income is tax free it uses up some of his basic-rate band, pushing £5,500 of his dividend income over the higher-rate threshold where it is taxed at 33.75%.*

Although Ollie's interest income is itself tax free it does have other tax consequences – it increases the income payable tax on his dividend income.

His interest income uses up £5,500 of his basic-rate band which means £5,500 of his dividend income will be taxed at 33.75% instead of 8.75%, an increase of 25%.

This means he will pay £1,375 more income tax (£5,500 x 25%).

Thus you could argue that he is effectively paying 25% tax on his 'tax-free' interest income.

### Example – Higher-rate Taxpayer

*Kenny is a company owner with a salary of £12,570, rental income of £20,000 and dividends of £40,000. He also has interest income of £2,000 (total income £74,570).*

*His rental income uses up his entire £5,000 starting-rate band. Because he is a higher-rate taxpayer he is entitled to a £500 personal savings allowance. So £500 of his interest income will be tax free, the remaining £1,500 will be taxed at 20%.*

*Kenny's interest income uses up £2,000 of his basic-rate band, pushing £2,000 of his dividend income over the higher-rate threshold where it is taxed at 33.75% instead of 8.75% – i.e. he pays 25% more tax.*

Kenny effectively pays 25% tax on his £500 of 'tax-free' interest income and 45% tax on the remaining £1,500 (20% on the interest directly and 25% additional dividend tax).

### *Example – Income over £100,000*
*Lynne is a company owner with a salary of £12,570 and dividends of £87,430 (total income £100,000).*

*At first glance it looks like she can enjoy £5,500 of tax-free interest. She does not have any taxable non-savings income that uses up her £5,000 starting-rate band. And as a higher-rate taxpayer she enjoys a £500 personal savings allowance.*

*Let's assume she now earns £5,500 of interest income. With an income of £105,500 she will lose £2,750 of her personal allowance which means £2,750 of her salary will now be taxed at 20%.*

*Because she has £2,750 of taxable non-savings income her £5,000 starting-rate band will be reduced to £2,250, so £2,250 of her interest income will be tax free.*

*And because she is a higher-rate taxpayer £500 of her interest income will be tax free thanks to the personal savings allowance.*

*The remaining £2,750 of her interest income will be taxed at 20%.*

*Her taxable salary income and interest income use up £8,250 of her basic-rate band which means £8,250 of her dividend income will be taxed at 33.75% instead of 8.75%.*

**In total, her £5,500 of interest income increases her income tax bill by £3,163. So far from being tax free you could say she is paying 57.5% tax on her interest income!**

Those whose existing income is in the £100-£125,140 bracket should think carefully about acquiring a new source of interest income.

## Additional-Rate Taxpayers

Once your income reaches £125,140 your personal allowance will be fully withdrawn and if you earn any more income you will become an additional-rate taxpayer and start paying 45% income tax on most types of income.

If you are a company owner with dividend income the tax rate increases from 33.75% to 39.35%.

The additional-rate threshold used to be £150,000 but has been reduced to £125,140. I suspect Taxcafe now has significantly more readers who are additional-rate taxpayers than a few years ago!

Additional-rate taxpayers do not receive any personal savings allowance but those whose income consists mainly of dividends can in theory benefit from the starting-rate band.

For example, a company owner who is an additional-rate taxpayer and whose income consists solely of interest and dividends can earn up to £5,000 of tax-free interest.

(In practice, the interest will not be tax free because it will use up some of your basic-rate band, pushing some dividend income over the additional-rate threshold where it will be taxed at 39.35% instead of 8.75%. So the effective tax rate is actually 30.6%.)

Most company owners who are additional-rate taxpayers will be paying themselves some salary income, or should be. A salary of at least £6,396 is required to protect your state pension entitlement.

As a result most will pay income tax on their interest income.

### Example
*Nikki is a company owner with a salary of £9,100 and interest income of £2,000. She also has £140,000 of dividend income.*

*She pays 20% tax on her interest income. Furthermore, her interest income uses up £2,000 of her basic-rate band so an additional £2,000 of her dividend income is pushed over the additional-rate threshold where it is taxed at 39.35% instead of 8.75%.*

*The presence of her interest income increases her tax bill by £1,012 so you could say she is paying 50.6% tax on her interest income.*

### Example
*Claudia is a company owner with salary and rental income of £60,000 which take her over the higher-rate threshold. She also has £140,000 of dividend income.*

*If she now earns £1,000 of interest income she will pay 40% tax on it. Furthermore, her interest income uses up £1,000 of her higher-rate band so an additional £1,000 of her dividend income is pushed over the additional-rate threshold where it is taxed at 39.35% instead of 33.75%.*

*The presence of her interest income increases her tax bill by £456 so you could say she is paying 45.6% tax on her interest income.*

### Example
*Isla is a company owner with salary and rental income of £130,000 which take her over the additional-rate threshold. She also has £140,000 of dividend income.*

*If she now earns £1,000 of interest income she will pay 45% tax on it. Her interest income does not affect the tax payable on her dividend income which is all taxed at the 39.35% additional rate whether she has interest income or not.*

*Isla therefore pays 45% tax on her interest income.*

## Summary

- Company owners who have very little or no taxable non-savings income can earn up to £6000 of tax-free interest.

- However, it's important to examine how earning interest income will affect the amount of tax you pay on your dividend income. Some of your dividend income may be pushed into a higher tax bracket.

# Part 3

# Making the Most of Tax-Free ISAs

# Chapter 8

# Cash ISAs

In the November 2023 Autumn Statement Chancellor Jeremy Hunt announced that the ISA allowance will remain frozen at £20,000 for the 2024/25 tax year which starts on 6th April 2024.

The allowance applies on a per person basis so couples can invest up to £40,000 per year.

Cash ISAs allow you to earn tax-free interest. You can choose between an easy-access ISA, that allows withdrawals at any time, or a fixed-rate ISA, which ties up your money for anything from one year to five years but will, hopefully, pay you more interest.

You can find the best ISA deals by searching "best cash isas" in Google. If you look below the sponsored ads you'll find various price comparison websites such as:

www.moneysavingexpert.com/savings/best-cash-isa

www.which.co.uk/money/savings-and-isas/isas/cash-isas

At the time of writing, interest rates of more than 5% were readily available.

At present the best easy-access accounts pay roughly the same amount of interest as the best one-year fixed-rate accounts.

They also pay more interest than three-year and five-year fixed rate accounts. In other words, at present you are punished for locking your money away for longer.

Longer fixes may, however, be worth going for if you expect interest rates to fall and want to lock in now.

Some other points to note:

- Many fixed-rate cash ISA products only allow you to add funds once, or within the first 30 days.

- Some easy-access accounts only allow around three penalty-free withdrawals per year.

- Price comparison websites don't always show the best deals. A local bank or building society may offer a better branch-based account.

## ISAs versus Regular Savings

Note, the best cash ISA interest rates are often lower than the best 'regular' savings account rates.

Of course, with an ISA the interest is guaranteed to be tax free whereas you could pay income tax on interest from a regular savings account if you exceed your personal savings allowance. (See Part 2 for more on how interest income is taxed.)

If you have to pay income tax on your interest income you will have to earn a much higher interest rate from a regular savings account to beat a cash ISA.

For example, if you can earn 5% from an ISA you would have to earn the following from a taxed savings account:

- 6.25% Basic-rate taxpayer        5% divided by  0.8
- 8.33% Higher-rate taxpayer       5% dividend by 0.6
- 9.09% Additional-rate taxpayer   5% dividend by 0.55

Interest rates this high are pretty much impossible to obtain.

Nevertheless, you may still prefer to not subscribe to a cash ISA and use all of your £20,000 allowance to invest in the stock market (see Chapter 10).

## Access to Your Money

Fixed-rate cash ISAs are more flexible than regular fixed-rate savings products when it comes to withdrawing money.

Most fixed-rate bonds, as they're typically called, do not allow you to withdraw any money before the end of the investment period, although you may be able to have your interest paid out.

With fixed-rate cash ISAs you are allowed to withdraw your money. There will typically be a penalty but you may sleep better knowing you can access your cash in an emergency.

The penalties for cash ISA withdrawals vary from bank to bank but are typically 90 days interest for one year fixes up to 365 days interest for five year fixes.

Note, you may not be able to make a partial withdrawal from your fixed-rate cash ISA – the bank may insist that you close your account.

Some banks do, however, allow you to make a few limited penalty free withdrawals.

With both easy-access ISAs and regular taxed easy-access savings accounts you can withdraw money at any time.

It may therefore be a good idea to spread your cash ISA savings across a range of easy-access and fixed-rate accounts.

## Multiple ISAs of the Same Type

In the November 2023 Autumn Statement Chancellor Jeremy Hunt announced that from 6th April 2024 you will be able to put money into more than one ISA of the same type each tax year.

At present you can put money in one cash ISA and also one stocks and shares ISA in the same tax year, as long as you stay within the £20,000 overall limit.

You can also put some of your £20,000 allowance in a Lifetime ISA (if you're age 18 to 39) or an Innovative Finance ISA.

But at present you cannot put money in two cash ISAs or three cash ISAs in the same tax year. You can only pay into one cash ISA with one bank. And you can only pay into one stock and shares ISA.

From 6<sup>th</sup> April 2024 you will be able to pay into more than one cash ISA with different banks. And you will be able to pay into more than one stocks and shares ISA.

Some banks allow you to split your £20,000 allowance between a mix of easy-access and fixed-rate products, all held under their roof.

For example, Charter Savings Bank has something called the Mix & Match ISA which allows you to put, say, £5,000 in their easy access cash ISA and perhaps later in the year deposit £10,000 in their one-year fixed-rate cash ISA product. If you have more money available after that you could top up your easy-access ISA or open a new fixed-rate product using the remaining £5,000 of your annual allowance.

However, not all ISA providers allow you to split your annual subscription in this manner, so removing the one cash ISA per year restriction from 6<sup>th</sup> April 2024 will give savers a great deal more flexibility.

You will be able to make full use your £20,000 ISA allowance by paying into a mix of easy-access and fixed-rate cash ISAs with different banks at different times during the tax year.

## Cash ISA Age Requirements

In the November 2023 Autumn Statement it was also announced that, from 6<sup>th</sup> April 2024, you will need to be 18 or over to open a cash ISA.

At present you can open a cash ISA if you are 16 or 17. This creates a small window of opportunity for 16 and 17 year olds to open adult ISAs before 6<sup>th</sup> April 2024.

(See Chapter 13 for more on children and saving tax on interest.)

## Flexible ISAs

Not all ISA providers offer flexible ISAs (it's not a requirement), so you may wish to check before you invest.

Flexible ISAs allow you to withdraw money and put it back during the same tax year, without affecting your £20,000 allowance.

For example, let's say you invest £20,000 in an easy-access cash ISA during the current tax year, using up your full allowance. Later on during the same tax year you find yourself needing some of this money and withdraw £10,000.

With a flexible ISA you can put that £10,000 back in again, as long as you do so before the end of the tax year on 5th April and as long as you put it back into the same account you withdrew it from.

With a non-flexible ISA you cannot put the money back in. The ISA provider will treat you as having already used up your £20,000 ISA allowance when you made the initial deposit.

As another example, let's say you have £50,000 of existing ISA savings and haven't made any new subscriptions during the current tax year. With a flexible ISA you could withdraw, say, £30,000 and put it back before 5th April plus an additional £20,000 to make use of this year's ISA allowance.

Flexible ISAs are most useful to those who want to keep their savings in easy-access cash ISAs.

They're also most useful to those who expect to use up most or all of their £20,000 ISA allowance each year. If your annual investment is much less than £20,000 you may not need the added flexibility, i.e. you may be able to add money, withdraw it and pay it back without going over the £20,000 annual limit.

## Cash ISA Transfers

You can transfer your existing ISA savings from one provider to another and this will not use up your £20,000 allowance for the current tax year.

For example, you may wish to transfer your stocks and shares ISA to a provider that charges a lower platform fee. I recently did this and was able to reduce the annual charge from 0.45% per year to 0.25%.

You may also wish to transfer your existing cash ISA savings to a bank or building society that offers a better interest rate.

The banks and building societies offering the best interest rates change continually. This means it is essential to shop around for the best deals.

For example, you may currently have your ISA savings in an attractive fixed-rate deal but the same bank may offer a much less competitive interest rate when your existing deal matures.

You can also transfer to a different type of ISA, for example from a cash ISA to a stocks and shares ISA.

You can transfer your ISA savings as often as you like.

Note, however, that what is allowed under the general rules will not always be allowed by every ISA provider.

Some of the banks and building societies that are paying the highest interest rates do not accept ISA transfers from other companies and will only accept new subscriptions.

However, many banks do allow you to transfer your existing ISA savings to them and will provide you with a fairly simple form to do this. You may be able to complete the form online but some banks insist that you post it or take it into a branch.

It's essential that you use your new ISA provider's transfer service. They will do all the work for you. You should NOT withdraw your savings from your old ISA and try to invest them with a new provider. If you take your savings out of the ISA wrapper they will lose their tax-free status.

Banks generally complete cash ISA transfers in 15 working days or less and some will pay you interest while your funds are being transferred.

Your current provider may levy a charge in the form of an interest penalty if your savings are currently in a fixed-rate account which hasn't reached maturity.

This charge could be worth paying if you are switching to a significantly higher interest rate. If not, you should perhaps wait until your existing deal matures before transferring.

Transferring money held in an easy-access ISA should be relatively straightforward and will often produce the greatest returns. Some banks pay paltry amounts of interest (for example 1.45%) on accounts that allow unlimited withdrawals, the best pay over 5%.

Generally speaking you don't have to transfer all your ISA savings to a new provider and most ISA transfer forms allow you to specify how much you wish to transfer.

However, your existing provider may not be as flexible and insist on a full transfer.

At present if you wish to transfer subscriptions you've made in the *current tax year* you have to transfer the whole amount of those current year subscriptions to your new provider.

You will still be able to pay into your new ISA: your old provider will tell the new one how much of your £20,000 allowance you have left. For example, if you've used £15,000 of this year's allowance before transferring, you'll still have £5,000 left to put into your new ISA.

For money you've invested in *previous tax years*, you can choose to transfer all or part of your savings.

In the November 2023 Autumn Statement it was announced that, from 6<sup>th</sup> April 2024, you will be able to make a partial transfer of cash you've invested in the current year to another provider. This change is in conjunction with the change that will allow you to contribute to more than one cash ISA every year.

# Chapter 9

# Money Market Funds

As interest rates have increased cash has poured into money market funds which now have around £250 billion of assets under management.

Most of this money is held by big companies and institutional investors. However, in recent times retail investors have been attracted to this space. According to the investment platform Interactive Investor, since December 2021 the number of its customers investing in money market funds has increased more than fourfold.

A money market fund may be an attractive place to park any cash you have sitting in your stocks and shares ISA or SIPP.

For example, you could keep your cash in a money market fund temporarily before deciding where to invest it for the long term.

Money market funds may also appeal to risk averse investors, looking for more stable returns and less volatility than stock market investments.

At the time of writing, some money market funds were yielding around 5.3% – tax free in an ISA or SIPP.

The returns are attractive when compared with bank accounts that give you easy access to your cash. You can normally get your hands on your money market cash within two to three days and there is no penalty for withdrawals.

Note the interest paid by money market funds fluctuates in line with short-term interest rates.

They'll typically try to beat a benchmark such as the Bank of England base rate or the Bank of England sterling overnight interbank average (SONIA). SONIA is the average interest rate banks pay to borrow money overnight from other financial institutions and is currently around 5.2%.

## Fees and Platform Charges

Although an interest rate of 5.3% may be attractive, from this you have to deduct fees, something you don't have to do with a regular savings account.

For example, the fund itself may have a fee of around 0.1% which isn't too bad but there will typically also be a 'platform fee' charged by your ISA or SIPP provider.

For example, Hargreaves Lansdown charges 0.45% per year on balances up to £250,000 so you could end up with a net return of around 4.75% after all fees have been deducted.

AJ Bell charges 0.25% per year on balances up to £250,000 so you could end up with a net return of around 4.95% if you use them.

Both platforms have lower fees for bigger accounts.

Other platforms have fixed fees. For example, Interactive Investor has plans which vary in price from £4.99 per month to £21.99 per month.

## Cash Held in a Stocks and Shares ISA

As an alternative to a money market fund you could simply hold cash in your stocks and shares ISA (or SIPP) and the investment platform will spread your money around various banks.

For example, Hargreaves Lansdown says: *"The majority of your money is held with core UK clearing banks such as Lloyds, HSBC, Bank of Scotland and Barclays. We carefully analyse each bank and move your money between them to help keep it safe – each bank is protected by the Financial Services Compensation Scheme (FSCS), so spreading your money around means you receive more protection."*

Platform fees aren't payable on cash balances but the interest rate is typically lower than from a money market fund.

The interest rates are sometimes different for ISAs and SIPPs.

For example, for ISA cash balances Hargreaves Lansdown currently pays 3.04% on the first £10,000 rising to 3.33% for cash balances of £100,000. (These are annual equivalent rates – see Chapter 3.)

For SIPP cash balances Hargreaves Lansdown currently pays 3.51% on the first £10,000 rising to 3.82% for cash balances of £100,000.

For ISA cash balances AJ Bell pays 1.96% on the first £10,000 rising to 2.42% for cash balances of £100,000. For SIPPs it pays 3.24% on the first £10,000 rising to 3.7% for cash balances of £100,000. These are the rates applying from April 2024.

With both Hargreaves and AJ Bell, those with more than £100,000 cash in their ISA or SIPP will receive a higher overall rate.

## What Investments Do Money Market Funds Hold?

A money market fund may have cash deposits with various banks, just as you and I would, but they also invest in assets that most small private investors don't have easy access to including:

- Certificates of deposit
- Commercial paper
- Floating-rate notes
- Short-dated bonds, including Government bonds

## Money Market Fund Risks

Unlike a regular savings account the value of your investment could go down. Money market funds are not protected by the Financial Services Compensation Scheme (see Chapter 2).

Some of the risks include:

- **Interest rate risk** – The value of any short-term bonds the fund holds could fall in value (even if only temporarily) if interest rates rise.

- **Default risk** – If one of the financial institutions with which the fund has money invested fails, the value of the fund may fall.

- **Liquidity risk** – During a market panic money market funds may experience liquidity issues – i.e. they may struggle to sell their investments quickly enough to meet investor redemptions. As a result the fund may have to suspend withdrawals temporarily. The Bank of England recently recommended that money market funds should increase their holdings of easier to sell assets that can be liquidated within one week.

Although money market funds are more risky than regular savings accounts they are still considered very low-risk investments.

A significant proportion of the investments will be of very short duration (a few months or less), which reduces the risk of capital losses arising from an increase in interest rates.

They typically hold a diversified portfolio of high-quality (for example AA) assets to reduce default risk and they hold money in bank deposits and very liquid Government bonds to reduce liquidity risk.

When it comes to accessing your cash this will typically take two to three days, sometimes a bit longer.

First you have to instruct the investment platform to sell all or part of your holding. This can take a day or two. Then you have to transfer the cash from the platform to your bank account. This can take around one day.

## A Sample Money Market Fund

To give you a flavour of what a well-managed money market fund looks like, let's take a closer look at the Royal London Short Term Money Market fund.

This is, of course, not a recommendation to buy and I suggest you consult a suitably qualified financial advisor.

The fund was launched in 1990 and now has over £6.5 billion under management. It's structured as an open-ended investment company (OEIC).

The fund is a 'short-term' money market fund, as opposed to a 'standard' money market fund. Standard money market funds can deliver higher returns by taking on more risk, for example by investing in longer-dated securities.

According to Royal London, the fund's objective is to preserve capital and provide an income by investing at least 80% in cash and cash equivalents.

The fund aims to outperform, after the deduction of charges, the Bank of England SONIA over a 12-month period.

It currently holds investments from 43 different issuers (mostly banks but also the UK Government) including the likes of Nationwide Building Society, DNB Bank (Norway's largest bank), Goldman Sachs, Societe Generale, KBC Bank (Belgian), Mizuho Bank (Japanese), Clydesdale Bank, ING Bank and Royal Bank of Canada.

The average maturity life of the investments is 31 days and the fund currently yields 5.33%.

The annual charge is 0.1% per year.

Between September 2020 and October 2021, during some of the financial upheaval of the Covid crisis, the unit price of the fund fell by 0.06%.

This was an extremely modest fall and the price recovered thereafter and has continued to rise ever since. Nevertheless it illustrates that, unlike a savings account, the value of a money market fund can go down and not just up.

# Chapter 10

# Cash ISA or Stocks and Shares ISA?

You can invest £20,000 per year in an ISA. You could put some of your allowance in a cash ISA and some of it in a stocks and share ISA – ideal for people who want to spread their money across both low-risk savings accounts and higher-risk stock market investments.

But what if you want to save *more* than £20,000 per year? Is it better to use your ISA allowance to earn tax-free interest or tax-free capital gains?

At first glance you should use your ISA allowance to earn tax-free interest because interest income is taxed much more heavily than capital gains.

If you are a higher-rate taxpayer you will pay 40% income tax on your interest income (aside from the first £500 which is tax free thanks to your personal savings allowance).

By contrast, you will only pay 20% tax on your capital gains, with the first £3,000 tax free thanks to your annual CGT exemption. (The annual CGT exemption is £6,000 for 2023/24 but falls to £3,000 on 6th April 2024.)

Although stock market capital gains are generally taxed much less heavily than bank account interest, my personal view is you should use your ISA allowance to invest in the stock market.

Although capital gains are taxed much less heavily than interest income I would want them sheltered in an ISA because I would expect my capital gains to be *much larger* than my interest income.

For example, if I can earn 5% from a savings account I would expect my stock market investments to generate annual returns of 10% or more.

I'm not for one minute saying that returns of 10% or more are easy to achieve. But why the heck would you risk losing your precious capital by investing in the stock market unless you expect to enjoy much higher returns?

If your stock market investments do produce much higher returns than your cash savings you could save more tax by sheltering your stock market investments in an ISA.

## Saving Income Tax on Dividend Income

There's another reason why using your ISA allowance to house your stock market investments may save you more tax in the long run: dividend income.

If you hold your stock market investments outside an ISA and are a higher-rate taxpayer you will pay 33.75% tax on your dividend income. (A small amount is tax free thanks to the dividend allowance: £1,000 in 2023/24, falling to £500 on 6th April 2024.)

Although 33.75% is less than the 40% paid on interest income, you would expect your dividend income to *grow* much faster than your interest income over time.

Put simply, it's better to pay 40% tax on £1,000 of interest income than 33.75% on £2,000 of dividend income.

So you could save income tax by keeping your stock market investments in an ISA.

## Tax Returns & Fees

One of the main reasons for holding your stock market investments in an ISA has nothing to do with saving tax and more to do with saving time and accountancy fees.

If you hold stock market investments outside an ISA you may have to report your sales to HMRC every year.

But if you hold your stock market investments in an ISA you can buy and sell shares to your heart's content and there will be nothing to report to the taxman.

If you're in the self assessment system you report your sales by completing the *Capital Gains Tax summary* pages of your tax return. There's a section for 'Listed shares and securities'.

You have to report the total number of disposals, the total disposal proceeds, allowable costs (which includes the initial purchase cost of your shares or funds), your total gains for the year and your total losses for the year.

If you don't sell any of your investments you will have nothing to report but if you are buying and selling shares and funds continually throughout the year this could be an extremely time-consuming exercise.

Investment platforms produce annual tax summaries which provide details of the sales you've made during the tax year and can make the job easier than it would be otherwise.

However, doing these calculations can get quite complicated, especially when you've bought and sold shares in the same company or fund at different times.

By contrast, taxable interest income is relatively easy to add up and report on your tax return.

## Who Has to Report to HMRC?

You generally have to report your stock market transactions if your total capital gains for the year exceed the annual exempt amount – £6,000 for 2023/24, falling to just £3,000 from 6th April 2024 onwards.

You may also have to report your sales if the total value of your disposal proceeds exceed £50,000, even if your gains are less than the annual exempt amount.

For those who don't normally complete a tax return, HMRC has also introduced a real-time reporting service that can be used to pay any outstanding capital gains tax.

# Chapter 11

# Innovative Finance ISAs

The innovative finance ISA (IFISA) was launched in April 2016 and allows investors to earn tax-free interest from "peer-to-peer" loans.

Peer-to-peer (P2P) loans are simply loans made by private individuals directly to other individuals and businesses. Many peer-to-peer loans are property related, providing bridging finance, buy-to-let loans and financing property developments.

Dedicated online platforms bring lenders and borrowers together.

P2P loans can also be made outside an ISA but, of course, the interest will then be taxable just like a regular savings account.

As with a traditional ISA, you can invest up to £20,000 per year in an IFISA. Your £20,000 allowance can be divided between a cash ISA, stocks and shares ISA, innovative finance ISA and lifetime ISA (if you're under 40).

And from 6th April 2024 you can subscribe to more than one of the *same type* of ISA during the same tax year.

For example, you can open, say, five innovative finance ISAs with different peer-to-peer lending platforms and contribute £4,000 to each. This may allow you to reduce the risk by spreading your investment across multiple platforms and loans.

It's also possible to transfer some or all of your existing ISA savings into a selection of innovative finance ISAs.

## How Much Interest Can You Earn?

Some of the peer-to-peer lending platforms advertise potential rates of around 7% or more, sometimes around 10%.

This is higher than what traditional banks are currently offering (typically no more than 5% on one year fixed rate deposits).

Why are the returns higher from peer-to-peer loans?

One argument is that, by cutting out the traditional middle man (the bank), it's possible to pay savers significantly more interest.

But of course the peer-to-peer lending platforms are themselves middlemen and take a cut, either directly or indirectly, from the borrowers and lenders who use the platform.

The main reason why the potential returns are much higher is because the risks are far greater.

Any potential interest rate being offered is merely a target return and is not guaranteed.

The higher the advertised rate of return, the higher the risk of losing some or all of your money.

## Peer-to-Peer Lending Risks

With a traditional bank account your savings are pooled with those of other savers and lent out to thousands, perhaps hundreds of thousands, of individuals and businesses.

If any of those borrowers default, the bank will absorb the loss and will not seek to reduce your account balance.

It's only in the event of mass defaults that a badly managed bank would be unable to repay its depositors.

These days banks are much more heavily regulated than they were before the 2008 financial crisis and, even if a bank were to fail, the UK Government guarantees deposits up to £85,000 per person per banking group (see Chapter 2).

In short, there is essentially no risk of losing your capital if you spread your savings across banks that are backed by the Financial Services Compensation Scheme.

The main risk you face is the erosion of the real value of your savings because of inflation. This is why savings accounts aren't very attractive long-term investments (especially if you have to pay income tax on your interest).

With peer-to-peer lending, however, your savings are not spread across thousands of different loans. You could be lending to a single borrower which massively increases your risk of losing money.

Furthermore, the loans you make are not covered by the Financial Services Compensation Scheme (in some cases the cash balance you hold with the platform itself before investing may be protected).

Some of the borrowers who turn to peer-to-peer platforms have been unable to obtain finance from traditional lenders and may therefore be inherently more risky than some of the blue-chip companies that borrow from banks.

Potential losses can be reduced by splitting your investment in peer-to-peer loans into small chunks and spreading your money across multiple loans. Some P2P platforms will do this for you automatically.

Some platforms also have contingency funds which are designed to pay out if a borrower defaults. These funds may not cover you if multiple borrowers default at the same time and will vary from platform to platform.

There are also peer-to-peer lending platforms that offer loans backed by property that can be sold to recoup any loan losses, although this would probably be a long drawn out process.

## Platform Risk

Another risk is that the peer-to-peer platform itself could go bust and there have been a number of high profile failures over the years, including the collapse of Lendy and Funding Secure in 2019.

If a platform fails, it could take years to get your money back and you may not get all of it back.

"Ring fencing" may protect the loans you have made directly to borrowers in the event of the platform going out of business. But at the very least you would probably expect significant delays while the mess is sorted out.

## Access to Funds

Peer-to-peer lending is not suitable for investors who need easy access to their savings.

You often have to commit to lending your money for a specific time period, typically anything from 12 months to three years.

During the period of the loan you may not be allowed to withdraw your original capital, or there may be fees and penalties if you require early access.

Some platforms allow you to sell your loans early through a secondary market. There may be a fee for this and there is no guarantee you will be able to find a willing buyer.

## Recent Changes to IFISAs

In the November 2023 Autumn Statement the Government announced that it has extended the scope of investments allowed in IFISAs from 6th April 2024 to include:

- Long-Term Asset Funds (LTAFs)
- Property Authorised Investment Funds (PAIFs) with extended notice periods

A long-term asset fund is a type of fund that lets you invest in long-term illiquid assets. These include infrastructure, real estate and private equity.

Property authorised investment funds are open-ended property funds that invest in either real property or the shares of UK real estate investment trusts (REITs).

Personally I don't think these investments will be attractive to most private investors as broadly similar, more liquid, investments can be purchased through a regular stocks and shares ISA.

## Taxcafe's View of IFISAs and P2P Loans

Peer-to-peer loans are sometimes described as a halfway house between putting your money in a traditional savings account and the stock market.

I'm not sure I agree with this point of view. I would regard investing in a big blue chip equity fund as less risky than investing in a portfolio of peer-to-peer loans. The value of the stock market fund could go down in the short term but I would be far less worried about any of the underlying companies going bankrupt.

Investing in peer-to-peer loans (via an innovative finance ISA or with taxable savings) may be a way to earn a higher return on a small percentage of your cash holdings.

However, it's important not to invest cash that you may require access to in the short term or even the medium term (because if a borrower defaults it may take a long time to recover your investment).

If you do decide to invest in peer-to-peer loans it's essential to have a diversified portfolio. It may be possible to achieve this by spreading your investment across multiple peer-to-peer lending platforms and loans.

Doing all the research to build a portfolio of peer-to-peer loans could be quite a time-consuming process and I'm not convinced the higher interest rates on offer are worth the effort.

## More Information

If you are interested in innovative finance ISAs and peer-to-peer loans an excellent resource is 4thway.co.uk

This website earns commissions from platforms if you sign up after clicking a link from the 4thway website. However, the website contains a wealth of information about P2P lending generally and the individual P2P platforms.

# Part 4

# More Tax Planning Ideas

# Chapter 12

# Using Pension Contributions to Pay Less Tax on Interest

If you have to pay income tax on your interest income one thing you can do to reduce the damage is make bigger pension contributions which enjoy tax relief.

This is especially the case if your interest income takes you over one of the key tax thresholds and you find yourself paying more income tax than you expected.

For example, you may find yourself paying 40% instead of 20% or 60% instead of 40%.

The key tax thresholds are:

- £50,270       Higher-rate threshold
- £100,000      Personal allowance withdrawal
- £125,140      Additional-rate threshold

In this chapter we'll take a look at some examples where taxpayers use their interest income to fund additional pension contributions.

Note, interest income does not count as *earnings* for pension contribution purposes. To make pension contributions you must generally have an equivalent amount of earnings, typically salary income or self-employment income.

For example, if you want to make a £10,000 gross pension contribution you must also have £10,000 of earnings.

Having said this, almost everyone can make a gross pension contribution of £3,600 per year, with £2,880 coming from you personally and £720 added to your pension pot by the taxman.

Note too in this chapter we do not cover all the pension rules which determine how much you can put in and how and when you can take money out. For more on pension tax issues please see the Taxcafe guide *Pension Magic*.

Let's start with someone who pays 40% tax on most of their interest income:

### *Example*

*Connor earns self-employment income of £60,000 and interest income of £2,000. As a higher-rate taxpayer the first £500 of his interest income is tax free and the remaining £1,500 is taxed at 40%, producing an income tax bill of £600.*

*If Connor uses his interest income to make an additional cash pension contribution of £2,000 the taxman will top this up with £500 of basic-rate tax relief, resulting in a gross contribution of £2,500.*

*His basic-rate band will be extended by the amount of his gross pension contribution which means £2,500 of his self-employment income will be taxed at 20% instead of 40%, saving him income tax of £500. This is his higher-rate tax relief.*

*In total Connor enjoys £1,000 of tax relief which is 40% of his gross pension contribution. His tax relief exceeds the income tax payable on his interest income.*

Although Connor is £1,000 better off overall, it's important to point out that he will have £1,500 less in his bank account to spend: he invested £2,000 of his own money in his pension but also received a tax 'refund' of £500 – his higher-rate tax relief.

The money in his pension is locked away until he reaches age 55 and in practice possibly for much longer because withdrawing money from a pension has various consequences, especially when you withdraw more than your tax-free lump sum.

So while Connor's pension contribution helps him save tax, it will have a negative effect on his cash flow. If Connor cannot afford to give up as much as £1,500 of disposable income he may prefer to make a smaller contribution.

When Connor eventually withdraws this money from his pension he will be able to take one quarter as a tax-free lump sum but will have to pay income tax on the remaining £1,875. If we assume he pays 20% tax when he retires the tax bill will be £375. Overall Connor will be £625 better off (£1,000 - £375) by making a pension contribution.

# Company Owners

As explained in Chapter 7, company owners can sometimes enjoy more tax-free interest than other people, sometimes as much as £6,000 per year.

However, it's possible your interest income will push some of your dividend income over the higher-rate threshold where it will be taxed at 33.75% instead of 8.75%. This is because dividends are always treated as the top slice of your income.

In this example a company owner makes a pension contribution so that none of her dividend income is taxed at 33.75%:

### *Example*
*Natalie is a company owner who pays herself a salary of £12,570 and dividend income of £37,700: total income £50,270. As a basic-rate taxpayer she pays just 8.75% income tax on all of her dividend income (except the small amount covered by her dividend allowance).*

*Let's say she inherits a cash lump sum, puts it in a savings account and earns £5,000 of interest income. Her interest income will be tax free thanks to her £5,000 starting-rate band (see Chapters 4 and 7).*

*However, her interest income uses up £5,000 of her basic-rate band. This means £5,000 of her dividend income will be pushed over the higher-rate threshold and taxed at 33.75% instead of 8.75%. This increases her tax bill by £1,250.*

*To avoid paying 33.75% tax Natalie makes a cash pension contribution of £4,000. The taxman adds £1,000 of basic-rate tax relief, resulting in a gross contribution of £5,000.*

*Natalie will also receive higher-rate tax relief: Her basic-rate band will be extended by £5,000 which means £5,000 of her dividend income will be taxed at 8.75% instead of 33.75%, saving her £1,250.*

*In total Natalie enjoys £2,250 or 45% tax relief on her £5,000 gross pension contribution.*

Like Connor in the above example, Natalie will end up with less cash in her personal bank account to spend. In her case she will have £2,750 less: she puts £4,000 into her pension but also receives £1,250 of higher-rate relief.

To save income tax moving forward Natalie could gradually invest the lump sum she inherited in an ISA. This will generate tax-free interest. She could also pay herself less dividend income to avoid paying tax at 33.75%.

If she wants to keep adding to her pension pot she can also consider getting her company to make the contributions instead.

(See the Taxcafe guide *Salary versus Dividends* for more information on this topic and the taxation of company owners generally.)

## Higher Contributions = Higher Savings Allowance

When you become a higher-rate taxpayer your personal savings allowance is reduced from £1,000 to £500 and when you become an additional-rate taxpayer it is reduced from £500 to zero.

It could be your interest income itself that tips the balance and makes you become a higher-rate taxpayer or additional-rate taxpayer.

Pension contributions can help in this situation because they reduce your *adjusted net income* which is the measure used to decide what type of taxpayer you are.

### *Example*
*Amanda has earnings of £50,000 and interest income of £2,000 – total income £52,000.*

*Remember the higher-rate threshold is £50,270 so Amanda has £1,730 of income above the threshold (£52,000 - £50,270).*

*As a higher-rate taxpayer she receives a personal savings allowance of £500 instead of £1,000. The first £500 of her interest income is tax free and the remaining £1,500 is taxed at 40%, which costs her £600.*

*However, If she makes a cash pension contribution of £1,384 (£1,730 x 0.8) the taxman will top this up with £346 of basic-rate tax relief to produce a gross pension contribution of £1,730.*

*Her adjusted net income is reduced by the amount of her gross pension contribution, so it falls from £52,000 to £50,270. As a basic-rate taxpayer she is now entitled to a personal savings allowance of £1,000.*

*How much tax will she pay on her interest income?*

*With £50,000 of earnings Amanda has £270 of her original basic-rate band remaining. And thanks to her pension contribution her basic-rate band will be increased by a further £1,730 so she now has £2,000 of basic-rate band remaining.*

*The first £1,000 of her interest income falls into her basic-rate band but is tax free thanks to her personal savings allowance. The final £1,000 will be taxed at 20%. The tax on her interest income falls to £200, a saving of £400.*

*In total Amanda enjoys a total of £746 tax relief on her £1,730 pension contribution (£346 + £400). In other words, she enjoys a total of 43% tax relief which is a bit more than the 40% tax relief most higher-rate taxpayers receive.*

## Income between £100,000 and £125,140

Once your income exceeds £100,000 your £12,570 income tax personal allowance is gradually taken away. It is reduced by £1 for every £2 you earn above £100,000. For example, if your income is £110,000 your personal allowance will be reduced by £5,000. If your income exceeds £125,140 you will have no personal allowance left at all.

The effect of having your personal allowance taken away is that most people earning between £100,000 and £125,140 face a hefty marginal income tax rate of 60%.

In other words, some taxpayers may effectively be paying 60% income tax on some of their interest income.

The flipside of this is that anyone in this income bracket who makes pension contributions can enjoy 60% tax relief.

Your personal allowance is only reduced if your 'adjusted net income' is more than £100,000. When calculating your adjusted net income you usually deduct any pension contributions you have made.

*Example*

*Ashley earns taxable interest income of £3,000. She also has other taxable earnings of £110,000. Total income: £113,000.*

*Because her interest income falls into the £100,000-£125,140 tax bracket she effectively pays 60% income tax on this income, except the first £500 which is tax free thanks to her personal savings allowance. The total tax on her interest income is £1,500.*

*If she uses her interest income to make a cash pension contribution of £3,000 the taxman will top this up with £750 of basic-rate tax relief, resulting in a gross contribution of £3,750.*

*Her basic-rate band will then be increased by £3,750 which means £3,750 of her other income will be taxed at 20% instead of 40%, saving her £750. This is his higher-rate tax relief.*

*Her pension contribution also reduces her adjusted net income by £3,750 which means £1,875 of her personal allowance is clawed back, saving her an additional £750 in tax (£1,875 x 40%).*

*In summary, her £3,750 gross pension contribution produces £2,250 of tax relief – a total of 60% tax relief!*

Although she enjoys a significant amount of tax relief, Ashley will end up with £1,500 less cash in her personal bank account to spend.

She personally puts away £3,000 into her pension but also saves £750 in tax thanks to her higher-rate relief and an additional £750 by clawing back some of her personal allowance.

## Summary

If you have taxable interest income you may be able to use that money to make pension contributions which enjoy tax relief of 40% or more.

In effect you may be able to claw back all the additional income tax you have to pay on your interest income in the shape of pension tax relief.

Although you may end up better off overall, it's important to remember that this may leave you with less cash in your personal bank account to spend.

Money in a pension can only be accessed from the age of 55 at present and there are other consequences when it comes to withdrawing anything over and above your tax-free lump sum.

# Chapter 13

# Using Your Children
# to Save Tax

If you are already making full use of your £20,000 ISA allowance and your £1,000/£500 personal savings allowance, you may be able to save income tax on interest income by simply giving money to your adult children.

(You could also give money to your spouse or partner if they are not making full use of their tax-free allowances – see Chapter 4.)

Adult children are those aged 18 or over.

They can stick the money in an ISA and enjoy tax-free interest (assuming they aren't already making full use of their own ISA allowance).

Even if they don't put the money in an ISA a total of up to £18,570 of their interest income may be tax free thanks to their:

- **£12,570 income tax personal allowance** – if your children have very little or no taxable income (for example if they're in full-time education) any interest income they earn could be tax free thanks to their personal allowance.

- **£5,000 starting-rate band** – even if your children have income that uses up their personal allowance they may still be able to earn up to £5,000 of tax-free interest thanks to the starting rate band (see Chapter 4).

- **£1,000/£500 personal savings allowance** – if your children are working full time and have other income that uses up their personal allowance and starting-rate band they may still be able to earn up to £1,000 of tax-free interest if they are basic-rate taxpayers (£500 if they're higher-rate taxpayers).

## How Much Tax Can You Save?

Let's say you're a higher-rate taxpayer with £20,000 of spare cash and you're already making full use of all your tax-free allowances, including your annual ISA allowance.

You could put the money in a taxed savings account in your own name earning, say, 5% per year. After paying 40% tax your after-tax return would drop to just 3%. Alternatively you could give the money to one of your children who can earn 5% tax free.

Assuming the interest is rolled up inside the savings account, after five years your taxed savings account would be worth £23,185. Your child's tax-free account would be worth £25,526, i.e. £2,340 more.

Gifting cash to your children could also help you save inheritance tax. There are a number of exemptions for lifetime gifts and even where these have been fully utilized the gift will fall out of your estate after seven years.

For a full discussion of inheritance tax issues I would refer you to the Taxcafe guide *How to Save Inheritance Tax*.


## But Should You Give Your Children Money?

Of course, saving income tax (or inheritance tax) is just one issue you have to consider when you give money to your children.

You must also be confident they will save the money rather than spend it!

Furthermore, although the *family* will be better off overall, you will be worse off personally if you give money away.

So this type of planning should only be considered by those who want to maximize the family's overall wealth, rather than focus on their own personal financial position.

If you are prepared to give money to your children, and your children are financially prudent, this type of family tax planning can be extremely powerful.

# Minor Children

Parents generally cannot give much money to children who are under 18 to earn tax-free interest.

Under the so-called 'settlements legislation' the child's income will be treated as the income of the parent if it exceeds £100 per year. All the interest (not just the amount over £100) will then be taxed in the hands of the parent who gave the money to the child.

You may be interested to know that this rule does not apply to children who are under 18 *and married*. However, under the Marriage and Civil Partnership Act 2022, 16 and 17 year olds in England and Wales are no longer allowed to marry. In Scotland and Northern Ireland 16 and 17 year olds are still allowed to marry.

For the rest of this chapter I will refer throughout to children who are under 18 and assume they are unmarried.

### *The £100 Rule*

The £100 rule is designed to prevent parents siphoning off money to their children to avoid income tax.

When interest rates were extremely low parents didn't have to worry about their children earning more than £100. These days a child with as little as £2,000 in a taxable savings account could trigger the anti-avoidance rule if the money came from just one of the parents.

Note the £100 limit applies separately to each parent and child.

For example, if a father deposits money in the bank accounts of his two minor children and each child earns, say, £90 interest, none of the interest will be taxed in the father's hands.

If the mother also deposits money in the children's bank accounts and each child also earns £90 interest on the money that came from her, the interest income will not be taxed in her hands.

The £100 rule also does not apply to gifts from grandparents or other people. In other words, children can earn more than £100 of interest income if the money in the bank account came from their grandparents or someone else other than their parents.

And because minor children can benefit from the £12,570 income tax personal allowance, the £5,000 starting-rate band and the £1,000/£500 personal savings allowance, any interest income they earn will in all likelihood be tax free.

If money is paid into a child's bank account by grandparents or others it may therefore be worth keeping hold of evidence that the payments were not made by the parents, in case you need it later on.

If parents do want to give their minor children cash, it may be better, where possible, if the gift comes from a lower-taxed parent, for example a parent who is a basic-rate taxpayer and does not personally use all of their own £1,000 personal savings allowance.

Parents can also open junior ISAs for their minor children. The income from these is not subject to the settlements legislation, i.e. it is completely tax free.

### Junior ISAs

Junior ISAs can be opened for any child who is under the age of 18.

A junior ISA has to be opened by a parent or guardian but anyone can pay into it. 16 and 17 year olds can open their own Junior ISAs.

Up to £9,000 can be invested in the junior ISA per tax year per child.

The money belongs to the child but they cannot access it until they turn 18. At that point the account will become an adult ISA.

You can choose between a cash junior ISA and a stocks and shares junior ISA or split the £9,000 allowance between both.

### Junior ISAs vs Children's Savings Accounts

Note although grandparents can pay into a junior ISA they can also pay into a grandchild's regular savings account.

Many banks have special children's savings accounts offering attractive rates of interest. These give the child access to their money (if that is what you want, if not a junior ISA may be better) and may offer a better interest rate than a junior ISA.

If the money comes from the grandparents the interest income will be taxed in the hands of the grandchildren, even if it amounts to more than £100 per tax year.

In most cases the interest income will be tax free in the hands of the child thanks to their income tax personal allowance, starting-rate band and personal savings allowance which together allow children without any other earnings to enjoy up to £18,570 per year of tax-free interest.

### Cash ISAs for 16 and 17 Year Olds

Children who are 16 or 17 can open their own adult cash ISAs, invest up to £20,000 during the current 2023/24 tax year and earn tax-free interest.

If their parents have opened a junior ISA on their behalf as well, a total of £29,000 can potentially be sheltered from income tax during the current tax year. Contributions can be made to the junior ISA until the child turns 18.

This loophole will close soon, however. In the November 2023 Autumn Statement it was announced that, from 6th April 2024, you will have to be 18 or over to open an adult cash ISA.

Before you give your 16 or 17 year old child up to £20,000 to open their own cash ISA remember the settlements legislation we mentioned earlier.

If the money to open the adult cash ISA comes from a *parent*, and the interest income exceeds £100, all the interest income will be taxed in the parent's hands while the child is under 18.

Just because the money is held in an ISA does not make it automatically tax free. The ISA regulations specifically exclude income from junior ISAs from the settlements legislation but other accounts are not exempt.

However, if the money to open the adult cash ISA comes from sources other than the child's parents (for example grandparents or a part-time job) the income will not be taxed in the parent's hands.

## Gifts to Other Family Members

There's nothing to stop you giving money to other members of your family to save income tax on interest income.

Children could even give money to their own parents. This is not something most people ever consider.

Such gifts may have adverse inheritance tax consequences because children generally outlive their parents. In other words, the gift you make to your parents may be subject to 40% inheritance tax before you get it back again! So in most cases giving money to your parents is probably a bad idea.

But inheritance tax isn't a problem for all individuals. If you are a high income earner and your parents have very modest assets that are unlikely to be subject to inheritance tax, gifting cash to them may allow them to earn tax-free interest and improve the family's overall financial position.

# Part 5

# Savings Platforms & Premium Bonds

# Chapter 14

# Savings Platforms: Making it Easy to Enjoy the Best Interest Rates

If you have spare cash that you would like to put in a savings account it's essential to shop around for the best interest rate.

**Note in this chapter we are talking about regular taxed savings accounts, not cash ISAs (Chapter 8 covers ISAs).**

In all likelihood the bank you use for your day to day banking will not be offering the best rates, especially when it comes to easy-access savings. For example my own bank currently pays just 1.75%, whereas rates of more than 5% are available elsewhere.

You can shop around for the best interest rates using a variety of excellent online resources like Money Saving Expert:

www.moneysavingexpert.com/savings/savings-accounts-best-interest

This website shows which banks are offering the highest interest rates for different account types (for example six-months fixed, one-year fixed and easy access). It also provides additional useful information to help you choose the right product.

Many of the top payers are small financial institutions that you may have never heard of, for example JN Bank, RCI Bank, and Hinckley and Rugby Building Society. However, the key point is that up to £85,000 of savings per person per banking group is covered by the Financial Services Compensation Scheme.

The bank paying the best interest rate today may not be offering the best rate in the future. To keep receiving the best deal you may have to keep opening new accounts with different banks.

Opening new accounts is relatively easy these days because you can do it all online. Where it can become time consuming is if you have to send the bank additional documentation to confirm your identify.

## Savings Platforms

One of the easiest ways to manage your savings is by using a savings platform such as Active Savings from Hargreaves Lansdown's or the Cash Savings Hub from AJ Bell.

These allow you to manage all your savings in one place and effortlessly transfer money from one bank to another, depending on who is offering the highest interest rate.

To explain how these platforms work let's take a closer look at Active Savings from Hargreaves Lansdown. I personally use this product so feel comfortable discussing it.

This is not a recommendation, however. The company has a reputation for excellent customer service but Active Savings is by no means perfect and two drawbacks include:

- **Bank choice** – at present you can access savings products from around 15 banks that have partnered with Hargreaves Lansdown. Better rates may be available from other banks.

- **Interest rates** – Hargreaves Lansdown does not charge you directly for using Active Savings, instead it charges the partner banks. This may result in the interest rates being slightly lower than if you went directly to the bank.

While the interest rates will not necessarily be the highest available, Active Savings makes it very easy to manage all your savings in one place and earn competitive rates of interest by switching easily from bank to bank.

## Opening Your Account

If you're an existing Hargreaves Lansdown customer you can open an Active Savings account almost instantly by logging on to their website:

www.hl.co.uk/investment-services/active-savings

If you are a new customer you can open your account online fairly quickly, although you may be required to provide further information to confirm your identity.

## Adding Money to Your Account

Once your Active Savings account is open the first thing you do is transfer money from your personal bank account to Hargreaves Lansdown's "cash hub". No interest is paid on cash hub balances, it's merely a place to temporarily hold cash before you pick a savings product. Money in the cash hub is held with Barclays.

You can add money to the cash hub using a debit card or by making a bank transfer. Bank transfers can be done quickly using a QR code which provides a secure link to your banking app.

## Savings Products Offered

Once your money is in the cash hub you can select a savings product, or several savings products at once.

At the time of writing the banks offering savings products included:

- Ratesetter (part of Metro Bank)
- Coventry Building Society
- Allica Bank
- Paragon
- Zopa
- Aldermore
- Close Brothers
- GB Bank
- Charter Savings Bank
- Icici Bank
- Santander International
- Emirates NBD
- Sainsbury's Bank
- Arbuthnot Latham
- Close Brothers

From these banks you can choose the following savings products:

- Easy access
- Limited access (for example, 4 withdrawals per year)
- 1 month fixed
- 3 months fixed
- 6 months fixed
- 9 months fixed
- 1 year fixed
- 18 months fixed
- 2 years fixed
- 3 years fixed
- 4 years fixed
- 5 years fixed

All the savings products are listed on a single easy to use page which shows you the interest rate offered, how often interest is paid and a "Details & apply" button.

Most of the easy-access accounts have a minimum investment of just £1 but many of the fixed-rate savings accounts require an investment of at least £1,000. Aldermore and Arbuthnot require deposits of £5,000 and £10,000 respectively.

Lots of additional information is provided for each savings product, for example how much interest you will earn after 12 months.

Once you've selected a savings product you simply enter how much of your cash hub balance you want to invest, tick a few declaration boxes and you're done. Hargreaves Lansdown will open the account for you with the bank.

## Managing Your Active Savings

You can open multiple savings accounts with different banks and these will all be displayed on your Active Savings Account page on the Hargreaves Lansdown website.

For example, you could open an easy-access account and a variety of fixed-rate accounts maturing on different dates.

Although you can view your Active Savings account in the Hargreaves app you cannot manage your savings there – you have to log into the website.

### *Easy-Access Accounts*

If you've chosen an easy-access account there will also be a button that lets you add money or withdraw money.

If you withdraw money it will go the cash hub first. You can then have it transferred to your personal bank account or you could, for example, invest it in a new easy-access account with one of the other banks, if that bank is now paying more interest.

It's important to note that a transfer to your personal bank account from an easy-access savings account held with Hargreaves Lansdown will probably take longer than a transfer from an easy-access account you have with the bank you use for your day to day banking.

For example, I also have an easy-access savings account linked directly to my current account. It doesn't pay much interest but I know I can transfer money to my current account instantly, including on weekends.

Withdrawals from Active Savings can take several days to complete, so you have to be careful about keeping any money there that you may need at very short notice.

Nevertheless an easy-access account does give you more access to your savings than a fixed-rate account, where no withdrawals are normally allowed until the product matures.

With all easy-access accounts the interest rate is variable which means it can be changed at any time. Hargreaves Lansdown will give you notice of any interest rate changes before they occur.

### *Fixed-Rate Accounts*

If you have some of your savings in a fixed-rate account, when the product matures your original deposit plus interest will be deposited in the cash hub, allowing you to open a new product with a different bank.

With fixed-rate accounts the interest rate is guaranteed for the whole period but withdrawals are usually prohibited until the product has matured.

With fixed-rate accounts the interest rate is normally higher the longer you are prepared to tie up your money. However, this is not the case at present.

For example, at the time of writing the best one year fixes were paying around 4.85% per year compared with 3.90% from three year fixes. So it may only be worth locking your money away in a longer-term product if you expect interest rates to fall.

## How Safe is Active Savings?

Under the Financial Services Compensation Scheme (FSCS) if a bank or building society fails up to £85,000 of your savings will be protected per banking group (see Chapter 2).

When your money is in a savings account opened through Active Savings your money is held by the bank or building society in question, not Hargreaves Lansdown.

In other words, you can hold more than £85,000 in Active Savings and be fully protected by the FSCS guarantee, as long as your money is adequately spread across different banks.

Money in the cash hub is held with Barclays. If Barclays were to fail, the FSCS will protect up to £85,000 of the money you hold in the cash hub. However, if you also hold money with Barclays outside of Active Savings, this may also fall under the same £85,000 limit.

# Chapter 15

# Earn Tax-Free 'Interest' from Premium Bonds

One way to earn tax-free "interest" is by putting some of your savings in premium bonds.

Premium bonds have been around since 1956 when they were introduced by former Chancellor Harold Macmillan to encourage people to save and rebuild Britain's post-war economy.

Over 21 million people now have around £120 billion tucked away in premium bonds, with an average investment of over £5,000.

Instead of paying interest, premium bonds offer cash prizes. However, unlike a traditional lottery, the Government promises to pay you back your original investment at any time (although its real value will have been eroded by inflation).

The prizes are paid out of the interest earned on the money people invest.

So premium bonds are sort of a cross between a savings account and a lottery. Like a savings account your initial stake is safe and, like a lottery, your returns are based on luck.

## Premium Bonds Snapshot

- They're available from the Government's National Savings & Investments (NS&I) – nsandi.com
- You can invest anything from £25 to £50,000
- You can cash in your bonds at any time (withdrawals take 3-5 days)
- They can be purchased for children under 16 (but only the nominated parent can manage and cash in the bonds)
- On the 1st of each month there's a prize draw
- Monthly prizes range from £25 to £1 million
- All prizes are tax free

# The Monthly Prize Draw

For every £1 you invest you obtain a unique bond number. Every month your numbers are entered in a prize draw.

Numbers are selected at random by ERNIE – NS&I's Electronic Random Number Indicator Equipment.

Apparently the latest version, ERNIE 5, is powered by "quantum technology" which is much faster than the old version which used "thermal noise" to produce random numbers!

You can check whether you have won using the prize checker app or online:

www.nsandi.com/prize-checker

In the January 2024 prize draw over £475 million was paid out in prizes as follows:

| Value of prize | Number of prizes |
|---|---|
| £1,000,000 | 2 |
| £100,000 | 91 |
| £50,000 | 182 |
| £25,000 | 365 |
| £10,000 | 912 |
| £5,000 | 1,821 |
| £1,000 | 19,020 |
| £500 | 57,060 |
| £100 | 2,363,105 |
| £50 | 2,363,105 |
| £25 | 1,037,784 |

Note, you need to hold your premium bonds for a whole month before they're entered in the prize draw. For example, if you buy bonds on, say, 5th March, they'll be eligible for the May draw.

To maximize the amount of bank interest you earn before you invest, it may be worth putting off your premium bond purchase until closer to the end of the month.

# The Annual Prize Fund Rate

As interest rates have gone up so has the total amount paid out. The annual "prize fund rate" was reduced from 4.65% to 4.40% in March 2024.

What this means is that for every £100 invested in premium bonds a total of £4.40 will be paid out in prizes each year.

A rate of 4.40% tax free is less than you can currently obtain from the best easy-access cash ISAs and the best regular easy-access savings accounts, which currently pay around 5%.

The interest you earn from a regular easy-access savings account could be tax free thanks to the £1,000/£500 personal savings allowance and ISA interest is, of course, always tax free.

But if you are already making full use of your ISA allowance and personal savings allowance, and would therefore pay income tax on any *additional* interest income you earn, a rate of 4.40% tax free is rather attractive.

You would have to earn the following interest rates from a regular taxed savings account to enjoy an after-tax return of 4.40%:

- 5.50%     Basic-rate taxpayers (paying 20% tax)
- 7.33%     Higher-rate taxpayers (paying 40% tax)
- 8.00%     Additional-rate taxpayers (paying 45% tax)

Rates this high are generally unavailable at present. Rates of just over 5% are available from the best-paying banks.

Many basic-rate taxpayers do not pay any income tax on their interest income: they do not save enough to max out the £20,000 ISA allowance or £1,000 personal savings allowance. Thus most can probably earn a tax-free return of around 5% (i.e. more than the 4.40% premium bond prize fund rate) by simply putting their money in a bank or building society account.

It's a different story for many higher-rate taxpayers and additional-rate taxpayers. These taxpayers are more likely to be making full use of their various tax-free allowances and would find it impossible to find a bank paying interest rates as high as 7.33% or 8.00% on their additional taxed savings.

We can therefore conclude that premium bonds are probably most attractive to higher-rate taxpayers and additional-rate taxpayers who are already making full use of their annual ISA allowance and personal savings allowance (additional-rate don't receive any personal savings allowance).

Furthermore, these are the individuals who are most likely to be able to afford to invest a significant amount of money in premium bonds, up to the maximum of £50,000.

The more premium bonds you own, the less luck plays a role and the greater your chances of earning a return closer to the prize fund rate.

## What Are Your Chances of Winning?

It's critical to point out that earning the quoted annual prize fund rate (4.40% from March 2024) is not guaranteed.

You could earn more than this or less than this, such is the nature of gambling. It's all about how lucky you are.

According to press reports, around three quarters of premium bond holders have never won a single prize!

The more you invest and the longer you hold your bonds the less luck plays a role but it still plays a big role.

Even if you have a substantial amount invested in premium bonds and enjoy average luck, you will probably not enjoy a return equal to the prize fund rate, which is skewed by the small number of big prizes that you are far less likely to win.

According to the website premiumbondsprizes.com, someone with £50,000 invested and average luck could expect to enjoy a tax-free return of 3.85%.

This falls to 3.5% with £10,000 invested and 0% with just £1,000 invested.

If you were to enjoy a tax-free return of between 3.5% and 3.85% from your premium bond investment this would still beat any taxed savings account if you are a higher-rate taxpayer or additional-rate taxpayer.

However, we have to emphasize that these returns are not guaranteed. You may enjoy less than average luck, in which case you will earn a lower return.

## Conclusion

Perhaps it's unfair to compare premium bonds to savings accounts because premium bonds also provide a lot of fun – you could win £100,000 or £1 million if you're extremely lucky.

And that is why so many people are attracted to them. Most of us like a wee flutter.

Premium bonds seem to make most sense financially if you're a higher-rate taxpayer or additional-rate taxpayer, make full use of your tax-free allowances but still want to keep some of your money in a cash-like investment that you can access at short notice.

Nevertheless, premium bonds should only form a small part of your overall investment portfolio. So if you want to increase your chances by investing tens of thousands of pounds, that money should still be a fairly insignificant part of your overall wealth.

Premium bonds should be seen as an alternative to cash-like investments that rarely keep up with inflation but nevertheless have their place in a balanced investment portfolio. But they are not an alternative to investing in growth assets that will hopefully beat inflation over time.

Finally, it's worth pointing out that, even if you do use up your ISA allowance and personal savings allowance, you can still enjoy tax-free returns by making pension contributions.

# Part 6

## Sole Traders & Company Owners

# Chapter 16

# Business Savings Accounts

Many business owners keep all their business cash in a current account earning no interest.

This didn't matter a few years ago. There was very little incentive to put your business cash in a savings account because the interest rates were so miserly – most easy-access savings accounts paid no more than 0.1%.

This has all changed now and it may be worth opening a dedicated savings account for your business.

Access will probably be a key consideration as most businesses have money continually flowing out to pay salaries and other expenses. It may be important that any cash kept in a savings account can be transferred almost instantly to your business current account.

For those businesses that have built up significant cash reserves there are savings accounts that pay higher fixed rates of interest if you're prepared to have your money locked up for a while.

## Sole Traders

### *Current Accounts*

A sole trader business does not have a legal identity separate from the owner.

Banks offer special business accounts that sole traders can use but there is no law preventing you from using an ordinary personal bank account for business purposes – you do not have to use a branded business account.

However, it's important to point out that your bank's terms and conditions will probably prohibit you from using an ordinary personal account for business purposes.

Whatever type of account you use, it's important to have a *separate* bank account for your business so that you can keep your personal and business finances separate.

Using a business account will help you monitor how your business is performing and separate personal and business expenses. This will make it far easier to complete your annual tax return.

Many business current accounts offer additional products and services that you may find useful, such as free accounting software and support from business managers.

Having a business account may also help you build up your business credit history which may make it easier to obtain a loan.

Most business current accounts charge fees, either a single monthly fee or a fee for every transaction.

For example, Barclays charges £8.50 per month which covers up to 500 electronic payments per month. There are additional charges for cheques and cash deposits and in-branch cash withdrawals (cash machine withdrawals are free).

RBS charges 35p for electronic payments into or out of your account and ATM withdrawals. Higher charges apply when you deposit cash or withdraw cash inside a branch.

Some banks offer free banking for, say, 24 months if you switch to them. This can be done fairly painlessly using the Current Account Switch Service.

You can compare some of the business current account offerings here:

www.moneysupermarket.com/current-accounts/business-bank-accounts

## Business Savings

It may also be a good idea to open a separate savings account for your business cash.

Sole traders pay income tax on their interest income just like any other individual taxpayer (see Part 2). Thus they can benefit from the £1,000/£500 personal savings allowance and enjoy tax-free interest.

Note there is no national insurance payable on interest income, even if it's earned in a business account.

At the very least you should consider opening an easy-access savings account that is linked to your business current account.

This will allow you to earn interest on some of your cash and regularly transfer it to your business current account to pay your bills.

You can check some of the interest rates on offer at the links below and compare them to what's on offer from your day-to-day banking provider:

www.moneyfactscompare.co.uk/business/business-easy-access-savings

www.money.co.uk/business/business-savings-accounts

In theory there's nothing to stop you opening an ordinary non-business easy-access savings account if it pays interest at a higher rate. However, some banks state in their terms and conditions that their personal savings accounts cannot be used for business purposes or cannot be linked to a business current account.

If you hold your business savings at a different bank, and immediate access is important, it's worth checking whether both banks allow "Faster Payments".

With Faster Payments withdrawals from your business savings account to your business current account should arrive in minutes, although apparently it can take up to two hours.

For example, Cynergy Bank explicitly states in its product documentation that it offers Faster Payments with its Business Saver account which currently pays 3.65%.

Charity Bank also says you can access your savings via Faster Payments but you have to first email a signed withdrawal notification form and this will be followed up with a call back and there is a limit of one withdrawal request per day.

If you require instant access to your business cash it may be preferable to keep your savings and current accounts under one roof, allowing you to go into your banking app and immediately transfer cash from your business savings account to your business current account.

You may end up earning less interest this way as many banks only pay around 1.5% on business easy-access savings accounts.

You have to be careful about storing too much cash in a business savings account at the expense of your current account. You don't want your current account going accidentally into the red. Some business owners may find it too time consuming to continually shift cash between accounts.

However, some business savings accounts, like the RBS Business Reserve account, have a 'sweep' facility that allows cash to be automatically transferred from your instant access savings account to your current account.

A feature like this allows almost all your business cash to be kept in the savings account earning interest.

### Longer-term Savings

If your sole trader business has built a significant cash reserve that you don't need for day-to-day payments you may prefer to invest it in an account that pays more interest, for example a fixed-rate bond.

Banks offer specific business savings products that accept deposits from both sole traders and limited companies.

However, as a sole trader you and the business are not legally separate so you may be able to withdraw surplus cash from your business current account and invest it in a regular savings account if it pays more interest.

You may also be able to withdraw surplus cash from your business account and place it in a cash ISA so that all your interest is guaranteed to be tax free.

If you think you may need to get your hands on your ISA savings it may be better to go for an easy-access ISA and one that is "flexible", allowing you to put back any money you take out without affecting your £20,000 allowance for the current tax year (see Chapter 8 for more on cash ISAs).

However, if you open a personal savings account to store your business cash watch out for those terms and conditions that state the account cannot be used for business purposes.

The small print may prevent you from, for example, linking an easy-access ISA to your business current account.

### *Sole Traders and FSCS Protection*

The bank accounts of sole traders are covered by the Financial Services Compensation Scheme (see Chapter 2).

However, if your business and personal accounts are held with the same bank you can claim up to £85,000 in total (not per account).

# Companies

Companies and their owners are separate legal entities. This means you cannot simply withdraw cash from your company's bank account and put it in a tax-free ISA or some other personal savings account that offers an attractive interest rate.

Any withdrawal of the company's cash will typically be treated as a salary payment, dividend or director's loan, with varying tax consequences.

If, however, the director's loan account is in *credit* (for example if the director has lent money to the company in the past) the credit balance can be withdrawn tax free. This may be worth doing if the company has sufficient cash and the director can earn more interest than the company or tax-free interest.

Companies pay corporation tax on their interest income. Under the new corporation tax regime a company could be paying anything from 19% to 26.5% tax on its interest income.

If the company's after-tax interest is then withdrawn as dividend income it will be subject to income tax in the hands of the directors at either 8.75% (basic-rate taxpayers), 33.75% (higher-rate taxpayers) or 39.35% (additional-rate taxpayers).

When you combine corporation tax and income tax, this means a company owner who is a higher-rate taxpayer could end up paying up to 51% tax on the company's interest income.

If you are a company owner and regularly pay yourself dividend income, one thing you could consider is paying yourself as much income as possible at the start of the tax year.

This is because it may be better if the same cash earns interest in your hands rather than the company's hands.

You may be able to earn a higher interest rate AND the interest income could be tax free in your hands thanks to either the £1,000/£500 personal savings allowance or the £5,000 starting-rate band (which company owners can sometimes benefit from – see Chapter 7).

And to the extent that you can put your dividend lump sum in an ISA, the interest income it generates is guaranteed to be tax free. (You may, however, prefer to use your ISA allowance to make stock-market investments.)

## *Company Savings Accounts*

Just like sole traders, companies can open savings accounts and earn interest income.

At the very least you should consider opening an easy-access savings account that is linked to your company's current account. This will allow your company to earn interest income on some of its cash and have money transferred regularly to its current account to settle bills.

Most banks will typically pay around 1.5% but rates of between 3% and 4% can be found by entering keywords like "best business easy-access accounts" into Google, which brings up websites like:

www.moneyfactscompare.co.uk/business/business-easy-access-savings

(See the above Sole Traders section for more information about business easy-access savings accounts as most banks offer the same account to sole traders and companies.)

If your company has built a significant cash reserve that you don't need for day-to-day payments you may prefer to invest some of this money in an account that pays more interest, for example a notice account or fixed-rate bond.

At present interest rates of around 5% are available if you shop around online using websites like:

www.moneyfactscompare.co.uk/business/business-notice-accounts

www.moneyfactscompare.co.uk/business/business-bonds

Most of the products listed on these websites are from banks you've probably never heard of before (I certainly hadn't!). You can compare what you find online with what's on offer from some of the better known high-street banks or your existing bank.

Some of the best interest rates on offer require a minimum deposit, for example £5,000 or even £50,000.

With notice accounts the interest rate is typically variable (it can go up or down) but is usually better than you'd get from an easy-access account because you have to provide notice to the bank before you can withdraw any money.

The notice period is typically anything from 30 days to 180 days. The longer the notice period, the higher the interest rate.

Fixed-rate bonds typically range from three months to five years. Remember with fixed-rate bonds you cannot withdraw any money before the end of the term. Five years is a long time to tie up your company's cash!

However, some company owners with significant cash reserves may be happy to lock up some of their company's cash for a year or so.

### Companies and FSCS Protection

Companies, just like private individuals, have their deposits protected up to £85,000 per banking group.

If your personal account is held with the same bank as your company's account, you can claim up to £85,000 for each account. This is because the company is treated as a separate legal entity.

### Potential Danger of Actively Managing Cash

When you sell your company or wind it up you could end up paying just 10% capital gains tax thanks to Business Asset Disposal Relief (previously known as Entrepreneurs Relief).

To qualify for Business Asset Disposal Relief, the company's main activities must be 'trading' related. If there is substantial non-trading activity you could be denied Business Asset Disposal Relief.

HMRC generally regards non-trading activities to be substantial where either non-trading income or non-trading assets exceed 20%

of the totals for the company as a whole. However, this is just a rule of thumb.

Non-trading activities may include holding too much cash and actively managing deposits.

In other words, if your company has a significant amount of cash, or actively manages its cash balances, there is a danger that you will be denied Business Asset Disposal Relief.

Like many aspects of tax law, this issue is something of a grey area and, in cases of doubt, professional advice is recommended.

# Chapter 17

# Tax-Free Directors Loans

## Borrowing From Your Company

Company owners can borrow money from their companies.

This can be a cheap way to get your hands on some cash for a short period of time.

In many cases the alternative would be to take additional dividend income, taxed at perhaps 33.75% or 39.35%. Or you could borrow money from a traditional lender and possibly pay a significant amount of interest.

I know one small business owner who recently borrowed £20,000 from his company to pay the stamp duty land tax bill on his new home. Several months later, when he turned 55, he withdrew some tax-free cash from his pension to repay his company.

Borrowing money from your company is often inexpensive but there are two potential tax charges:

- a 33.75% tax paid by the *company* (the section 455 charge)
- a benefit-in-kind charge paid by the *director*

### The 33.75% Tax Charge

When small company owners borrow money from their companies a tax charge of 33.75% may become payable by the company if the loan remains outstanding for too long.

This tax charge is designed to prevent company owners taking all their income as loans instead of taxable dividends (33.75% is the same rate higher-rate taxpayers pay on their dividends).

The good news is that, even if the 33.75% tax charge does become payable, it will be refunded after the loan is repaid. The company will be repaid nine months after the end of the accounting period in which the loan is repaid.

Another bit of good news is that short-term loans escape the 33.75% tax charge: it does not have to be paid if the loan is repaid within nine months of the end of the company's accounting period.

### *Example*

*Billy's Brickies Ltd has an accounting period that ends on 31st December 2024. The company makes a £10,000 loan to Billy, the sole shareholder and director, in July 2024.*

*Billy repays the loan before the end of September 2025. The company will not have to pay the 33.75% tax charge because the loan was repaid within nine months of the end of the accounting period in which it was made.*

## The Benefit-in-Kind Charge

If the loan is an interest-free loan the director will have to pay income tax on what's known as a benefit in kind.

The company will also have to pay employer's national insurance on the benefit. There is, however, no employee's national insurance payable by the director.

The benefit in kind that is added to your income is calculated using the Government's 'official rate of interest' which is currently just 2.25% per year.

This is dirt cheap compared with the actual interest rates charged by banks and other lenders.

For example, for an interest-free loan of £20,000 for one year the director will have the following benefit in kind added to his taxable income:

£20,000 loan x 2.25% = £450

A higher-rate taxpayer director will typically pay up to 45% income tax on this benefit so the overall cost to him will be no more than £203:

£450 x 45% = £203

(See Chapter 7 for an explanation as to why the income tax rate could be up to 45%.)

The company will also have to pay class 1A national insurance of £62:

$$£20,000 \text{ loan x } 2.25\% \text{ x } 13.8\% = £62$$

Employer's national insurance is a tax-deductible expense, so the net cost would be no more than £50 (£62 less 19% corporation tax relief).

Having to pay a total of £253 per year to borrow £20,000 from your company is, in my opinion, a pretty good deal!

Note too that your accountant will probably also charge a fee to complete a P11D form to report the benefit of an interest-free loan to HMRC. If the company already has other benefits to report, however, reporting one more may not cost very much.

The benefit in kind is reduced if there is a formal obligation to pay interest to the company. If the director pays interest at 2.25% or more there will be no benefit in kind charge.

### Why So Cheap?

Back in 2009 the official rate of interest was 6.25%. Despite the recent surge in UK interest rates, the official rate has so far only increased from 2% to the current level of 2.25%.

Why it has remained so low is a bit of a mystery. If the official rate were to increase to say 6% the tax cost of directors' loans could almost triple. In other words, loans to directors may become more expensive in future, possibly from April 2024.

### Loans for £10,000 or less

Some loans are exempt from benefit-in-kind charges.

There is no benefit-in-kind charge if all loans to the director total £10,000 or less throughout the tax year. (Note, all amounts due from the director to the company have to be counted here.)

Although the loan may be exempt from benefit-in-kind charges, the 33.75% company tax charge still has to be paid if the loan is not repaid on time.

Nevertheless, this exemption allows a company owner to take a loan of up to £10,000 for up to 21 months with no adverse tax consequences.

And when the company is run by a couple a total of up to £20,000 can be borrowed tax free.

**Further Information**

This section provides just a brief overview of loans to directors.

For a more complete discussion, with lots more interesting examples, please see the Taxcafe guide *Salary versus Dividends*.

## Lending Money to Your Company

In the previous section we looked at loans from the company to the director. In this section we'll look at the opposite scenario: loans from the director to the company.

If your company owes you money you can make it pay you interest. In some cases, the interest will be both a tax-deductible expense for the company and tax free in your hands: the best case scenario when it comes to extracting money from your company.

The interest income you receive from your company could be tax free thanks to the £5,000 starting-rate band and £1,000/£500 personal savings allowance (see Chapter 7).

Even if income tax is payable on your interest income it will typically be taxed less heavily than other types of income you can extract from your company.

Salaries beyond a certain level are subject to national insurance as well as income tax and the combined tax rates on dividend income (corporation tax and income tax) are higher than the income tax rates that apply to interest income.

## Practical Issues

There are lots of circumstances in which company owners may lend money to their companies. For example, it may be a new company that needs some cash to get started or a well-established company that needs money to buy some new equipment.

In some cases company owners lend money to their companies indirectly, for example when a dividend is declared but the cash is not withdrawn immediately, perhaps because the company owner wants to reinvest it to help the business grow.

There is no requirement for a director to charge interest on a loan to their own company but, if they do, it must not exceed a reasonable commercial rate.

Interest paid to a director will usually be a tax deductible expense for the company, as long as the money is used for business purposes.

One major drawback of getting your company to pay you interest is the company will have to deduct income tax at 20% and pay this to HMRC for each quarter in which interest is paid, using form CT61.

To ease the admin burden interest could be paid annually, during the quarter to 31st March.

The company should also issue the director with an annual interest certificate.

If deducting 20% tax results in a tax overpayment, the director can reclaim the excess via their self-assessment tax return.

## How Much Tax Can You Save?

This will depend on how much income you earn and what type of income you earn.

### Example 1
### Basic-Rate Taxpayer, No Taxable Non-Savings Income
*Gillian is a company director with salary and other non-savings income (e.g. rental income) of £12,570. She has £15,000 of dividend income. She charges her company £5,000 interest for a substantial loan she made to help it buy new equipment. Interest is at a commercial rate.*

*The interest will be a tax deductible business expense, saving the company at least £950 corporation tax (£5,000 x 19%). Gillian has no taxable non-savings income, so all of her interest income will be tax free, being covered by the £5,000 starting-rate band (although the company will initially have to withhold 20% tax and pay this to HMRC).*

*If instead Gillian decided to NOT pay herself interest, the company would have an extra £5,000 of taxable profit. After paying at least £950 corporation tax there would be an extra £4,050 at most that could be paid out as dividends taxed at 8.75%, leaving Gillian with £3,696.*

*The potential tax saving is at least £1,304 (£5,000 versus £3,696).*

### Example 2
### Higher-Rate Taxpayer, No Taxable Non-Savings Income
*As before Gillian has £12,570 of salary and other non-savings income and £5,000 of interest from her company. However, this time she has dividend income of £50,000, some of which is taxed at 33.75%.*

*Gillian can enjoy £5,000 of tax-free interest income thanks to her starting-rate band. But because her starting-rate band uses up £5,000 of her basic-rate band an additional £5,000 of her dividends will be taxed at 33.75% instead of 8.75%, resulting in additional tax of £1,250. So, effectively Gillian receives £3,750 after tax (£5,000 - £1,250).*

*If she did not pay herself interest, the company would have an extra £5,000 profit. As the company is already paying dividends of £50,000, it is reasonable to assume it will have a marginal corporation tax rate of 26.5%. Hence, after corporation tax, there would only be £3,675 remaining to pay out as further dividends. This would leave Gillian with just £2,435 after paying 33.75% income tax.*

*Hence, for a higher-rate taxpayer with no taxable non-savings income the maximum potential saving is £1,315 (£3,750 versus £2,435).*

*The saving will be less where the company has a lower marginal corporation tax rate. However, even at the lowest possible corporation tax rate of 19%, there would be a saving of £1,067 in this scenario.*

### Example 3
### Higher-Rate Taxpayer, No Starting Rate Band Available
*This time Gillian has £17,570 of salary and rental income, £5,000 of interest income and £50,000 of dividend income.*

*Because she has £5,000 of taxable non-savings income (£17,570 – £12,570 personal allowance) she will have no starting-rate band available.*

*However, thanks to the personal savings allowance, £500 of her interest income will be tax free and the rest will be taxed at 20%, leaving her with £4,100.*

*An additional £5,000 of her dividend income will be taxed at 33.75% instead of 8.75%, resulting in additional income tax of £1,250. So effectively Gillian ends up with £2,850 after tax.*

*If instead she had decided to not pay herself interest, the company would have an extra £5,000 of taxable profit. After paying 26.5% corporation tax, there would only be £3,675 remaining to pay out as further dividends. This would leave Gillian with just £2,435 after paying 33.75% tax.*

*In this case Gillian is £415 better off paying herself interest (£2,850 versus £2,435).*

The tax saving will be less if the company has a lower marginal corporation tax rate, but it would still be £366 if the company is paying tax at 25% and, even in the unlikely event that the company's corporation tax rate is only 19%, there remains a saving of £167.

## Summary

Some company owners may be able to save over £1,000 by getting their companies to pay them interest.

The potential tax saving is a lot smaller if there is no starting-rate band available, for example if the taxpayer has a significant amount of salary income or rental income.

For many taxpayers the additional tax paperwork will nullify the tax savings, although this burden can be significantly reduced by making a single, annual interest payment.

Finally, it's important to remember the interest you charge your company must not exceed a fair commercial rate.

For further information see the Taxcafe guide *Salary versus Dividends*.

# Part 7

# Earn Tax-Free Interest by Paying Off Your Debt

# Chapter 18

# Paying Off the Mortgage on Your Home

Paying off your personal debt is a great way to earn tax-free interest.

For example, if the interest rate on your home mortgage is 6% and you reduce the debt by £100, you will save yourself £6 per year in interest.

Saving money is pretty much the same as earning it, so saving £6 is pretty much the same as earning £6 tax free.

Put another way, if the interest rate on your mortgage is 6% you will effectively enjoy a tax-free return of 6% on any money used to reduce the debt.

Reducing debt is an attractive alternative to putting money in a savings account because:

- Borrowing rates are generally higher than savings rates – saving 6% is better than earning, say, 4%.

- You may have to pay income tax on the interest you earn in a savings account. But the interest you save by reducing your personal debt has no adverse tax consequences. In other words, saving £6 is much better than earning £4 and paying 40% tax which would leave you with just £2.40.

## Early Repayment Charges

Making mortgage overpayments is not always practicable. There may be early repayment penalties, especially if you are currently on a fixed-rate deal.

These typically range from 1% to 5% of the overpayment, depending on how many years into the deal you are.

For example, if you're on a five-year fixed rate you could be charged 5% on any overpayments in year one, 4% in year two, 3% in year three, 2% in year four and 1% in year five.

So if you're in year four of a five-year deal and make a £10,000 overpayment you could be charged £200: £10,000 x 2%.

With two-year fixes the early repayment charge is often 2% in year one and 1% in year two but some lenders have higher charges.

Early repayment charges usually come into play when you pay off your entire mortgage part way through the fixed-rate period, for example if you sell your home and move to another lender.

However, many lenders allow you to make some overpayments while you are on a fixed rate.

Typically they will allow you to make overpayments of up to 10% of your outstanding mortgage balance each year.

The precise amount you can overpay will vary from lender to lender. For example, it may be 10% of the amount outstanding on the 1$^{st}$ of January. So if your mortgage balance was £100,000 on the 1$^{st}$ of January this year, you may be able to make an overpayment of £10,000 this year.

If you are no longer on a fixed-rate deal, and paying your lender's standard variable rate, you will normally be allowed to make unlimited overpayments without any early repayment charges.

Early repayment charges vary from lender to lender so it's important to check your mortgage documentation and speak to them before you start making any overpayments. This way you can find out exactly how much of your mortgage you can pay off without incurring a charge.

## Another Benefit of Mortgage Overpayments

Apart from earning tax-free interest, reducing your mortgage balance may allow you to access a better mortgage deal.

This is because smaller mortgages are less risky for lenders, so they may be willing to reward you with a lower interest rate.

Lenders measure this risk using something called the loan to value ratio (LTV) which compares the size of your mortgage with the value of your home. The smaller this number is, the less risky the loan.

LTV is calculated by dividing the amount of your mortgage by the value of your home. So if your mortgage is £80,000 and your home is worth £100,000, the LTV is 80%.

If you pay off £5,000 you will have a mortgage balance of £75,000 and the LTV will fall to 75%.

(I'm assuming here that the value of your home remains the same, something that is by no means guaranteed.)

How much could a lower LTV reduce the interest rate on your mortgage?

Looking at some results from a well-known price comparison website, reducing the LTV to 75% would enable you to access two-year deals with an average interest rate of 4.89%, compared with 5.33% when the LTV is 80%.

LTVs typically work in percentage bands, so if you pay off enough of your mortgage to move into a lower band, you could qualify for a better deal.

A few years ago my own fixed-rate deal was coming to an end but my mortgage was just a few hundred pounds too large to qualify for the bank's best fixed-rate deal. So while I was on the phone to the bank's mortgage advisor I made the small overpayment that was required to bring my LTV down to the required level, allowing me to access the lower interest rate and enjoy significant savings over the next couple of years.

Below are some examples of interest rates on offer at different loan to value ratios. In each case I've taken the average of the five cheapest lenders' rates from a well-known price comparison website.

In each case it's the average interest rate for two-year fixes that have no mortgage arrangement fee. These fees are often around £1,000 or more.

| LTV | Interest rate |
|-----|---------------|
| 95% | 5.80% |
| 90% | 5.49% |
| 85% | 5.41% |
| 80% | 5.33% |
| 75% | 4.89% |
| 70% | 4.89% |
| 65% | 4.89% |
| 60% | 4.76% |

The average interest rate falls by over one percentage point as the LTV ratio drops from 95% to 60%. However, in some cases the savings you will enjoy by moving into a lower LTV band will be very modest.

There is no fall in the average interest rate when the LTV drops from 75% to 65%. However, when I performed the same calculation a few months earlier there was a small reduction – the mortgage market is constantly changing!

It's also important to point out that your existing lender may not offer a better interest rate when your LTV falls by a few percentage points.

In other words, you may have to move lender to access a better deal. This is often more time consuming and difficult than simply taking a new fixed-rate deal with your existing lender.

An LTV of 60% is one of the lowest you can have when it comes to securing the best mortgage deal. Some lenders may offer mortgage rates for lower LTVs such as 50% and even 40%. This is where knowing a good mortgage broker could come in handy.


## Alternatives to Reducing Your Home Mortgage

There are other things you can do with your savings including:

- Keeping the money in a tax-free savings account
- Paying down other personal debts (e.g. credit card debt)
- Paying down buy-to-let mortgages

We will examine these alternatives in the next three chapters.

# Chapter 19

# Paying Off Your Mortgage vs Tax-Free Savings

At the beginning of the previous chapter I stated that reducing your home mortgage may be an attractive alternative to keeping money in a savings account because mortgage interest rates are generally higher than savings account rates.

This is almost always the case if you are paying your bank's standard variable rate which could be around 7% or more at present.

If you are subject to your bank's standard variable rate you may be able earn a tax-free return of 7% or more by paying down your mortgage. It's pretty much impossible to find a savings account paying this much interest.

But if you are able to access a new fixed-rate mortgage the interest rate will be far lower. For example, at the time of writing, rates of between 4.5% and 5% were being offered by many lenders for two year fixes.

If you then use your savings to reduce such a debt you would enjoy a tax-free return of between 4.5% and 5%.

At the time of writing it was also possible to find cash ISAs paying between 4.5% and 5%. In other words, you may be able to earn a similar tax-free return from a cash ISA.

And you may be able to earn a much higher return from a cash ISA if you locked in a low mortgage interest rate before rates started rising.

A couple of years ago a friend of mine took out a five-year fixed rate mortgage with an interest rate of just 1.8%. If she uses her savings to repay some of this debt she will currently enjoy a tax-free return of just 1.8%.

She should perhaps consider keeping her money in a cash ISA until her fixed-rate deal comes to an end and the interest rate on her mortgage increases.

The advantage of keeping your money in an ISA is you retain access to your cash. When you plough money into your mortgage you generally lose access to it completely (although it may be possible to remortgage at some point).

With easy-access cash ISAs you can withdraw money whenever you like.

With fixed-rate cash ISAs the interest rates are often higher but there are penalties if you withdraw money early. For example, the bank may charge you an amount equivalent to 180 days interest if you withdraw money early from a two-year fixed ISA.

But if you're willing to pay the penalty you can still access your cash in an emergency and if you can wait until the end of the fixed-rate period you will obtain full access to your savings again.

In summary, at the time of writing, you may be able to earn a higher tax-free return by sticking your savings in a cash ISA, instead of using them to reduce your mortgage.

Although the *lowest* mortgage interest rates are very similar to the *highest* cash ISA interest rates you may have to shop around for the best deals. For example, some banks only pay around 1.75% on easy-access cash ISAs.

## What if You've Used up Your ISA Allowance?

What if you are already making full use of your £20,000 ISA allowance but still have additional savings you would like to put in a savings account or use to repay some of your mortgage?

First of all it's worth stating that your spouse or partner can also invest £20,000 per year in an ISA. If they haven't made full use of their allowance it may be worth transferring cash to them.

Adult children and grandchildren also have their own ISA allowance so you may wish to consider transferring cash to them so that they can earn tax-free interest (see Chapter 13).

If you want to invest in a stocks and shares ISA it's important to remember that you can pay into both a stocks and shares ISA and a cash ISA in the same tax year, as long as you don't invest more than £20,000 in total.

For example, you could invest £10,000 in one and £10,000 in the other or £5,000 in one and £15,000 in the other.

See Chapter 8 for more on cash ISAs, including recent changes to the rules.

### *Taxed Savings Accounts*

If you are making full use of your ISA allowance you may have to put any additional savings you have in a regular savings account, which could be an easy-access or fixed-rate account (sometimes called a fixed-rate bond).

The best regular savings accounts often pay more interest than cash ISAs, apparently because ISAs are more expensive to administer.

The bad news is regular fixed-rate savings accounts generally do not allow any withdrawals until the product matures, although you may be able to have your interest paid into a separate bank account. By contrast, fixed-rate cash ISAs let you access your cash, even if this means paying a penalty.

If you are nervous about tying up your savings you may wish to go for an easy-access account or a fixed-rate account that lasts for less than 12 months. It's possible to fix your interest rate for anything from just one month to five years.

The other disadvantage with regular savings accounts is your interest is potentially subject to income tax.

Your interest may still be tax free thanks to the £1,000/£500 personal savings allowance or £5,000 starting-rate band (see Chapter 4).

However, if you are already making full use of these tax-free allowances you will have to pay income tax on any additional interest income you earn.

For example, at the time of writing it was possible to earn around 5.2% from the best one year fixed rate accounts. As a higher-rate taxpayer you would pay 40% tax which means your after-tax return would fall to just 3.12%.

If the interest rate on your mortgage is more than 3.12% you will currently enjoy a higher return by using any spare savings you have to reduce your mortgage debt.

However, if having access to your savings is a priority you may wish to keep your money in a savings account, even if this means earning a lower return.

# Chapter 20

# Paying Off Other Personal Debts

You can also use your savings to reduce any personal loans, credit card debt and other short-term borrowings you have.

This will often produce the highest tax-free returns of all, better than putting your money in a cash ISA, better than paying off mortgages and better than paying off any business borrowings.

This is for two reasons:

- **High interest rates**. The interest rates on personal loans, overdrafts, credit card debt and the like are usually much, much higher than savings accounts and mortgages.

- **No tax relief**. Unlike loans used for business purposes, the interest payable on personal borrowings does not enjoy any tax relief. This makes personal loans more expensive than business loans.

For example, at the time of writing one online lender was quoting an interest rate of 27.1% for a personal loan of £7,500 for 36 months. There was also an upfront fee of £360 payable, which bumps up the 'annual percentage rate' (APR) to 31.6%.

(The APR is a key number when comparing different loans because it includes both interest and fees.)

If you used some of your savings to repay such a loan you would enjoy a tax-free return of 27.1% per year.

Most personal loans are less expensive than this. According to the Bank of England, the average interest rate on new personal loans to individuals is currently 9.05%.

The average interest rate on interest-charging overdrafts is currently 22.45% and the average interest rate on credit cards is 20.94%.

This means that the average borrower who uses his or her savings to repay such loans will enjoy tax-free returns ranging from 9.05% to 22.45% per year.

For example, if you have £1,000 of credit card debt and use your savings to pay it off you could save over £200 in interest per year. You will effectively be earning over 20% per year tax free.

That's much higher than the £50 or so you would earn by keeping your savings in even the best cash ISA.

## Early Repayment Penalties

As with mortgages, there may be early repayment penalties when you repay personal borrowings early.

Many personal loans can be repaid early, as can credit cards and overdrafts. There may be early repayment fees or penalties if you pay off car finance early.

It's important to check your loan documentation or speak directly with the lender.

## Personal Borrowings with Low Interest Rates

It's possible the interest rate you are paying on your personal borrowings is currently *lower* than the interest rate you can earn on your cash savings.

This would be the case if, for example, you have a credit card with a low introductory rate.

In such cases it may be worth keeping your cash in a tax-free savings account until the interest rate on your personal borrowings increases.

# Chapter 21

# Paying Off Buy-to-Let Debt

You can also use your savings to pay down any buy-to-let mortgages you have.

Buy-to-let mortgages are generally more expensive than home mortgages. So at first glance paying off buy-to-let debt could save you more money.

However, because buy-to-let mortgages also enjoy tax relief, you may find that it's the mortgage on your home or other personal debt which is more expensive and should therefore be repaid first.

As a general rule it's better to reduce your personal debt before you reduce your business debt because business debt enjoys tax relief and is therefore cheaper.

Of course you also have to compare interest rates. If the interest rate on your business debt is high enough it may be worth paying off your business debt first, even though it enjoys tax relief.

## Tax Relief Restrictions

Unlike other business owners, residential landlords who are higher-rate taxpayers or additional-rate taxpayers do not enjoy full tax relief on their interest payments.

Instead of enjoying 40% or 45% tax relief, as a landlord you receive a 20% tax 'basic-rate tax reduction' which is deducted from your income tax bill.

Let's say you have a £100,000 buy-to-let mortgage and the interest rate is currently 6%. You'll be paying £6,000 per year in interest and will be entitled to a basic-rate tax reduction of £1,200.

The true after-tax cost of your interest payments is therefore £4,800 which is equivalent to an interest rate of 4.8%.

Thus, if you can earn more than 4.8% elsewhere (for example from a tax-free savings account or by paying off the mortgage on your home) you may wish to consider doing that instead.

## Mortgage Prisoners

In recent times there have been many reports of landlords becoming 'mortgage prisoners'.

Lenders apply a variety of stress tests when assessing buy-to-let applications. The rental income from the property must be sufficiently high to pay the mortgage interest, including an additional marginal of safety in case interest rates increase.

These tests became more difficult to pass as interest rates increased.

As a result some landlords have struggled to obtain new fixed-rate deals when their existing deals have come to an end. They have then become trapped paying their existing lender's standard variable rate which could be around 9%.

After taking account of the 20% tax relief that applies to buy-to-let mortgages the after-tax cost of a 9% interest rate is 7.2%.

Landlords who find themselves in this situation may therefore be able to enjoy an after-tax return of around 7.2% by reducing their buy-to-let debt.

## Other Factors to Consider

There are lots of factors to consider beyond a simple comparison of headline interest rates.

For example:

- As with home loans, there could be early repayment charges when you reduce a buy-to-let mortgage before any fixed-rate deal has come to an end, although many buy-to-let lenders also allow overpayments of up to 10% per year.

- You may prefer to pay down mortgage A instead of mortgage B even though the interest rate on mortgage A is currently lower. You may expect the interest rate on mortgage A to increase sharply in the near future when that property's current deal comes to an end.

- You may also prefer to pay down buy-to-let mortgage A if this reduces the loan to value ratio enough to let you access a better deal.

- You may prefer to keep any spare cash you have in a savings account to cover any unforeseen property expenses, such as property repairs.

In summary, landlords need to be very careful about sinking their precious cash into their mortgages. You have to think about your future mortgage expenses and other property expenses.

## Loan Arrangement Fees

Buy-to-let mortgages often come with relatively low interest rates but large arrangement fees. The largest arrangement fees are typically a percentage of the amount borrowed.

For example, some lenders charge as much as 3% or 5% of the amount borrowed and sometimes as much as 7%. So for a £100,000 mortgage the arrangement fee could be anything from £3,000 to £7,000.

Fortunately, these mortgage arrangement fees also attract 20% tax relief. So a fee of £3,000 has an after-tax cost of £2,400.

Some landlords have been forced to take out deals with high arrangement fees in order to pass their lender's affordability criteria.

Mortgage arrangement fees can be added to the amount borrowed rather than paid up front, if this additional borrowing is acceptable to the lender. Interest will then be payable on the fees that are added to your mortgage balance.

Adding arrangement fees to your mortgage helps with monthly cash flow but also means that this significant additional cost is often swept under the carpet.

When you come to the end of your fixed-rate deal you may be forced to take out another fixed-rate deal and pay another round of loan arrangement fees. Otherwise you'll be forced to pay your lender's standard variable rate which could be around 9% at present.

If you have an interest-only mortgage, as most landlords do, repeatedly adding loan arrangement fees every few years will result in a steady increase in your mortgage debt which could eventually affect your ability to remortgage.

It's important to point out that not all buy-to-let mortgages have large arrangement fees calculated as a percentage of the amount borrowed. For some the loan arrangement fee is a fixed amount (such as £995) and it's possible to obtain buy-to-let mortgages with no loan arrangement fees.

Often these work out cheaper in the end, even though the monthly interest payments are higher.

## Calculating the After Tax Cost of Buy-to-Let Debt

Mortgage arrangement fees have to be included when calculating the after-tax cost of a buy-to-let mortgage:

### Example

*Jean has an interest only buy-to-let mortgage of £100,000 and takes out a new two-year fixed rate deal. The initial rate is just 4% but the mortgage comes with an arrangement fee of 5% (£5,000) which she pays up front.*

*She expects she will have to take out a similar deal at the end of the two-year period.*

*Over the two year period she pays £8,000 interest and £5,000 in fees, a total of £13,000 or £6,500 per year. So she is effectively paying 6.5% per year, not 4%.*

*As a residential landlord Jean will enjoy 20% tax relief on her mortgage interest payments and her loan arrangement fees, so the annual after-tax cost of the loan is:*

*£6,500 less 20% tax reduction = £5,200*

*With a mortgage of £100,000 this is equivalent to an after-tax interest rate of 5.2%.*

Looking at her position in very simplistic terms, if Jean has spare savings and uses them to reduce her mortgage debt before she takes out this fixed-rate deal she will enjoy an after-tax return of 5.2% over the next two years.

That's an attractive return but there may be more appealing alternatives. She could currently earn around 4.5% from a two-year cash ISA – a lower return but this would allow her to retain access to her savings. She may need those savings to pay future loan arrangement fees or other property expenses.

Having said this, if she uses her spare savings to reduce her buy-to-let debt, this may reduce the loan to value ratio enough to allow her to access a better mortgage deal.

It's a tricky decision!

## Preserving Your Cash

From a strict comparison of after-tax interest rates, you may be better off using any spare cash to reduce your buy-to-let debt.

Although paying off debt may be optimal on paper it's also prudent to maintain a healthy cash reserve to protect against unexpected drops in rental income and unforeseen expenses.

The problem with using spare cash to reduce a mortgage is the money essentially disappears into a black hole and you normally can't get it back easily. A mortgage is not the same as an easy-access savings account!

You may be able to remortgage but that will take time and incur additional costs.

# Chapter 22

# Paying Off Business Debt

Sole traders can claim tax relief for their interest costs, including interest payable on:

- Bank loans and other business loans
- Overdrafts
- Credit cards
- Hire purchase payments

## How Much Interest Do Business Owners Pay?

Some types of business borrowing are more expensive than others.

For example, unsecured loans (where no collateral is provided) are typically more expensive than secured loans.

The most expensive types of borrowing (for both small business owners and other individuals) are typically overdrafts and credit cards, with interest rates ranging from roughly 15% to 20%.

Other business loans have interest rates that vary significantly according to a whole range of different factors, for example the size of the loan, how the loan is used, the length of the loan and whether the interest rate is fixed.

Some lenders advertise rates of around 6% but a rate of around 12% would not be uncommon.

Some business loans also have arrangement fees (for example 5% of the amount borrowed) which can increase the cost significantly.

## Is My Interest Tax Deductible?

In this chapter we will examine whether self-employed business owners should use any surplus cash they have to repay their business debt early.

We will assume that all their interest payments enjoy full tax relief.

This means their interest payments will reduce their taxable profits and therefore reduce the amount of income tax and national insurance they have to pay.

Interest payments are typically tax deductible if the loan is used for business purposes.

However, for a detailed examination of the tax deductibility of interest payments I would recommend reading the Taxcafe guide *Small Business Tax Saving Tactics* which goes into a lot more detail.

At present any trading business that uses the so-called cash basis is limited to a maximum annual claim of £500 for interest on cash borrowings (business loans and overdrafts). Other interest costs, such as hire purchase interest, mortgage interest on business premises, and credit card interest on business purchases are generally allowable.

However, in the November 2023 Autumn Statement the Government announced that, from 2024/25 onwards, the £500 restriction will be relaxed.

## Repaying Business Borrowings Early

Should you use any surplus cash you have to repay your business borrowings?

(Many lenders allow business loans to be repaid early but you should always check whether there are any early repayment charges.)

On the one hand, business loans are cheaper than many other types of borrowing because the interest enjoys full tax relief.

On the other hand, many business loans (like many personal loans) have high interest rates.

To answer the question we have to weigh up these two conflicting factors and the easiest way to do that is with an example.

### Example

*Kathleen is a sole trader and a higher-rate taxpayer. This means her marginal tax rate is 42% (40% income tax and 2% national insurance).*

*She has a £12,500 business loan on which 8% interest is payable: £1,000 per year. Her interest enjoys tax relief of £420 per year (£1,000 x 42%), so the after-tax cost is just £580 per year. This means the loan is actually costing her 4.64% per year, not 8% (£580/£12,500 x 100).*

*Let's say she has £12,500 of spare cash and is trying to decide whether to repay her business loan or put the money in a cash ISA paying 5% tax free.*

*If she uses the money to repay the loan she will save £580 per year. By contrast, if she puts the money in an ISA she will earn £625 of tax-free interest (£12,500 x 5%).*

*Kathleen will be £45 better off keeping her spare cash in an ISA.*

### Example Revised

*The facts are exactly the same except this time we will assume the interest rate on the loan is 12% per year which means her annual interest payment is £1,500.*

*Her interest payments enjoy tax relief of £630 per year (£1,500 x 42%) so the after-tax cost is £870 per year. This means the after-tax cost of the loan is 6.96% (£870/£12,500 x 100).*

*If she uses her spare cash to repay the loan she will save herself £870 per year. By contrast if she puts the money in an ISA earning 5% she will receive £625 of tax-free interest.*

*Kathleen will be £245 per year better off if she repays her business loan.*

Of course, when making a decision such as this there are lots of other factors to consider. For example, Kathleen may still prefer to keep her spare £12,500 in a cash ISA so that it can be used to cover any unforeseen personal or business expenses.

# Comparing After-Tax Interest Rates

To help decide whether business borrowing are worth repaying early you have to first calculate the cost of the loan net of tax relief (income tax and national insurance).

Sole traders face the following marginal tax rates in 2024/25, depending on their profits:

- 26%   Basic-rate taxpayers            £12,570-£50,270
- 42%   Higher-rate taxpayers           £50,270-£100,000
- 62%   Personal allowance removed £100,000-£125,140
- 47%   Additional-rate taxpayers     £125,140+

Thus the after-tax cost of a business loan can generally be calculated as follows:

- Basic-rate taxpayers                  Interest rate x 0.74
- Higher-rate taxpayers                 Interest rate x 0.58
- Personal allowance withdrawal   Interest rate x 0.38
- Additional-rate taxpayers           Interest rate x 0.55

For example, for a loan with an interest rate of 10% the after-tax cost would be:

- Basic-rate taxpayers                  10% x 0.74 = 7.4%
- Higher-rate taxpayers                 10% x 0.58 = 5.8%
- Personal allowance withdrawal   10% x 0.38 = 3.8%
- Additional-rate taxpayers           10% x 0.55 = 5.5%

These after-tax rates can then be compared with the return you could earn by using the money for another purpose such as:

- Investing in a cash ISA (tax-free interest)
- Paying down a home mortgage (no tax relief on interest)
- Paying down other personal debt (no tax relief on interest)
- Paying down buy-to-let debt (20% tax relief on interest)
- Investing in taxed savings (e.g. if no spare ISA allowance)

## Example

*Chloe is a sole trader and higher-rate taxpayer. She has £10,000 of spare cash and is trying to decide whether to use the money to:*

- *Invest in a cash ISA*                4% tax free
- *Invest in taxed savings*             4.5% (2.7% after 40% tax)
- *Reduce her home mortgage*            5% no tax relief
- *Reduce a personal loan*              8% no tax relief
- *Reduce a buy-to-let loan*            6% (4.8% after 20% tax relief)
- *Reduce a business loan*              10% (5.8% after 42% tax relief)

*It's important that Chloe ignores the headline interest rates and compares after-tax interest rates. Chloe will obtain the most bang for her buck by directing her spare cash towards the savings product or loan that has the highest after-tax interest rate.*

*The highest return is obtained by reducing her personal loan because there is no tax relief on those interest payments. The second highest return is obtained by reducing her business loan, then the mortgage on her home.*

However, Chloe should think carefully about using her spare cash to reduce her debts because she may then lose access to precious cash. By contrast, cash kept in a savings account can generally be accessed fairly easily.

When making decisions such as these it is also important to look further ahead than just one year. This is because interest rates change continually. Directing spare cash towards the debt or savings product that offers the highest after-tax return today may not turn out to be the optimal decision in the future.

# Chapter 23

# Company Owners with Business Premises

Many company owners own their business premises *personally* and the company pays them rent.

Paying yourself rent is often more tax efficient than paying yourself a higher salary because there is no national insurance on rental income. Paying yourself rent is also generally more tax efficient than paying yourself dividend income (see the Taxcafe guide *Salary versus Dividends* for a full discussion of this issue).

Many company owners who own their business premises also have a mortgage on the property and personally pay the interest.

These interest payments will normally enjoy full tax relief and can be offset against your taxable rental income.

Although the tax relief on *residential* property mortgages is restricted (see Chapter 21), mortgages used to buy *commercial* properties generally enjoy full tax relief.

## Repaying Business Borrowings Early

Should you use any surplus cash you have to repay the mortgage over your business premises?

Because this type of mortgage interest enjoys full tax relief you could say this is one of the best types of debt to have and should therefore not be repaid early.

Many company owners who are higher-rate taxpayers will be enjoying 45% tax relief on their interest payments.

For example, if the interest rate on the mortgage is 7% the true after-tax cost (net of 45% tax relief) will be just 3.85%:

$$7\% \times 0.55 = 3.85\%$$

Thus if you use any spare cash to reduce such a mortgage you will effectively earn a return of just 3.85% per year.

You may be better off using spare cash to repay any personal debts you have, where the interest rate charged exceeds 3.85% and there is no tax relief.

You may also be better off keeping your cash in a savings account if you can tax-free interest of more than 3.85%.

For example, if you can earn 5% tax free from a cash ISA you would have to be paying *more* than 9.09% on your business premises mortgage to make paying down the debt more attractive.

This is because the after-tax cost of a mortgage with an interest rate of 9.09% is exactly 5%:

$$9.09\% \times 0.55 = 5\%$$

To make it worthwhile to withdraw cash from your ISA and pay down this debt the mortgage interest rate would have to exceed 9.09%.

For example, in the unlikely event that the interest rate on your mortgage is as high as 12%, the interest cost net of tax relief would be 6.6%:

$$12\% \times 0.55 = 6.6\%$$

In this case it may be worthwhile using your savings to pay down your mortgage because 6.6% is a better return than 5%.

Of course, as stated throughout this guide, you should always think twice about using your precious cash reserves (especially your ISA savings which take time to build) to pay down debt.

And you should always think beyond the interest rates you are currently paying or earning. Interest rates on both mortgages and savings change continually.

Earlier I stated that many company owners who are higher-rate taxpayers enjoy 45% tax relief on their mortgage interest. To understand why this is the case let's look at an example:

### Example

*Harry is a company owner and a higher-rate taxpayer. He pays himself a salary of £12,570 and takes most of his remaining income as dividends.*

*He owns his business premises personally and has an outstanding mortgage of £100,000. The interest rate is currently 7% which costs him £7,000 per year.*

*The company pays him rental income of £12,000 per year, so he has a taxable rental profit of £5,000 (£12,000 - £7,000).*

*Harry also has £100,000 of ISA savings earning 5% tax free, i.e. £5,000 per year.*

*Harry wants to know whether he will save money by withdrawing his savings and paying off his mortgage.*

*If he pays off his mortgage and no longer has any mortgage interest his taxable rental profit will increase by £7,000. He will pay 20% income tax on this additional income: £1,400.*

*Note, although Harry is a higher-rate taxpayer he only pays 20% tax on his rental profit because it falls into his basic-rate band. In his case it is only his dividend income that is subject to higher-rate tax (dividends are always treated as the top slice of income).*

*Because his additional rental profit will use up £7,000 of his basic-rate band, an additional £7,000 of his dividend income will be pushed over the higher-rate threshold where it will be taxed at 33.75% instead of 8.75%. In other words, he will pay an additional 25% tax on £7,000 of his dividend income: £1,750.*

*In total, Harry's rental profit goes up by £7,000 but his income tax bill increases by £3,150. He effectively pays 45% tax, both directly and indirectly, on his additional rental profit.*

This is why I stated earlier that many company owners enjoy 45% tax relief on their mortgage interest payments. Before Harry paid off his mortgage his interest payments were reducing his rental profits and saving him 45% tax.

By paying off his £100,000 mortgage Harry is left with £3,850 more after-tax rental income (£7,000 - £3,150).

Thus he will enjoy an after-tax return of 3.85% by paying off his mortgage (£3,850/£100,000 x 100).

This is why I stated earlier that, if the interest rate on your business mortgage is 7%, you will effectively earn a return of 3.85% on any money you use to reduce it.

However, we still haven't answered Harry's question: will he save money by using his ISA savings and paying off his mortgage?

He is currently enjoying tax-free interest of £5,000 per year from his ISA. Paying off his mortgage will leave him with £3,850 more after-tax rental income.

Thus Harry will be £1,150 per year *worse off* if he pays off his mortgage.

## Shortcut Calculation

For taxpayers in a similar situation to Harry the saving or loss that can be enjoyed by using savings to repay debt can be calculated quickly by comparing after-tax interest rates.

For example, we know that Harry's mortgage is costing 7% but just 3.85% after deducting 45% tax relief:

$$7\% \times 0.55 = 3.85\%$$

We also know that he is earning 5% tax free in an ISA.

The difference between 3.85% and 5% is 1.15% which means Harry will lose 1.15% on any cash used to repay his mortgage. Thus if he uses all his £100,000 savings to repay his mortgage he will be £1,150 worse off.

Let's say instead that Harry is only earning 4% tax free in his ISA and his mortgage is costing 9%, 4.95% net of tax relief:

$$9\% \times 0.55 = 4.95\%$$

The difference between 4.95% and 4% is 0.95%. So if Harry uses, say, £20,000 of his savings to reduce his mortgage he will save £190 per year (£20,000 x 0.95%).

## Taxed Interest Income

In the above example we assumed that Harry had £100,000 in an ISA earning tax-free interest.

But what if he always makes full use of his ISA allowance yet still has additional non-ISA savings on which the interest is fully taxable?

Should he take some of these taxed savings to repay the mortgage on his business premises?

Again we have to compare after-tax interest rates. Let's say his mortgage interest rate is 7% and he is earning 5% on his taxed savings.

If he takes, say, £10,000 out of his taxed savings account and uses it to reduce his mortgage his taxable income will increase by £200.

This is because his interest bill will fall by £700 (£10,000 x 7%), *increasing* his rental profit by £700, and his savings interest will *decrease* by £500 (£10,000 x 5%).

He will pay 20% tax on this additional income: £40. His additional income will also use up £200 of his basic-rate band which means an additional £200 of his dividend income will be taxed at 33.75% instead of 8.75%. Additional tax: £50.

Harry's after-tax income will increase by £110 (£200 - £40 - £50) if he uses his savings to reduce his debt.

(Note, to keep the example simple we have ignored the fact that Harry can enjoy £500 of tax-free interest thanks to his personal savings allowance – we'll assume the allowance is used up by his remaining savings.)

## Comparing After-Tax Interest Rates

The saving or loss that can be enjoyed by using taxed savings to repay debt can be calculated quickly by comparing after-tax interest rates.

We know that Harry's mortgage costs 3.85% after deducting 45% tax relief:

$$7\% \times 0.55 = 3.85\%$$

Similarly, he effectively pays 45% tax on his interest income and therefore earns an after-tax return of 2.75%:

$$5\% \times 0.55 = 2.75\%$$

Because his mortgage is costing him 1.1% more than he is earning from his savings, paying down his debt produces a higher overall return.

As long as the interest rate on his mortgage is higher than what he can earn in a taxed savings account he will save money by repaying some of his mortgage.

## Not All Taxpayers Are Like Harry!

Although many company owners, like Harry, may be enjoying 45% tax relief on their mortgage interest payments, company owners come in many shapes and sizes.

For example, some will have much more income than Harry and some will have much less and the composition of that income may vary considerably. For example, some may have much higher rental income and some may have no dividend income at all.

For this reason it is essential to do your own calculations to determine how much you will save or lose by paying off any business mortgage you have over your premises.

And finally it's important to stress that if you use your savings to reduce your debt you may lose access to precious cash. In some cases it may be worth keeping hold of your savings, even if you are enjoying a lower after-tax return.